Reframing the
Leadership Landscape

This book is a must read because in our world problems have acquired a wicked nature, they are complex. So leaders need to bear in mind that solutions can only be found through collaborative approaches.

> *Elizabeth Filippouli, Founder and CEO of Global Thinkers Forum (GTF)*

In the complex context in which companies now operate, leaders must leave their comfort zones and become more multi-disciplinary, requiring new skills and approaches.

This book tries to draw the threads together, while also raising relevant questions about sustainable wealth creation and the need for a more collaborative capitalism.

> *David Nicol, Chief Executive Officer, Brewin Dolphin Limited*

Leading for sustainable success demands much more than maintaining a lifetime of traditional learning. It also requires the understanding of new disciplines that themselves adapt as global society changes. This well written book very readably highlights this tension and leads the way in promoting the changes required to maintain business growth and profitability.

> *Professor John Board, Dean, Henley Business School*

Reframing the Leadership Landscape

Creating a Culture of Collaboration

ROGER HAYES and
REGINALD WATTS

 Routledge
Taylor & Francis Group

LONDON AND NEW YORK

First published 2015 by Gower Publishing

2 Park Square, Milton Park, Abingdon, Oxon OX14 4RN
711 Third Avenue, New York, NY 10017, USA

Routledge is an imprint of the Taylor & Francis Group, an informa business

First issued in paperback 2016

British Library Cataloguing in Publication Data
A catalogue record for this book is available from the British Library.

Library of Congress Cataloging-in-Publication Data
Hayes, Roger.
    Reframing the leadership landscape / by Roger Hayes and Reginald Watts.
        pages cm
    Includes bibliographical references and index.
        ISBN 978-1-4724-5870-4 (hardback : alk. paper) – ISBN 978-1-4724-5871-1 (ebook) – ISBN 978-1-4724-5872-8 (epub)
    1. Corporate culture. 2. Interpersonal relations. 3. Leadership. 4. Globalization. I. Watts, Reginald, 1932- II. Title.

    HD58.7.H417 2015
    658.4'095–dc23

2014044635

ISBN: 978-1-4724-5870-4 (hbk)
ISBN: 978-1-138-22809-2 (pbk)

Contents

Dedication
Dr Millicent Danker (1950–2013)

This book is not advocating the abolition of capitalism, if indeed that were possible. It is not arguing for the state to do more, rather that both should collaborate further for everyone's benefit. Capitalism has won the battle of ideas against state control and witnessed the collapse of centrally planned regimes. It has created untold wealth and rising middle classes. Yet free-market liberalism remains unpopular, despite the importance of wealth creation and respect for private property, because it is unstable and unequal. In short capitalism is not trusted, because rather than the pursuit of narrow self-interest and short-termism, it should be based on collaboration and shared values. A more inclusive approach would surely enhance its moral legitimacy? While it may be susceptible to reform, it is not so much about legislation, rather attitude and culture change.

This is the stakeholding thesis as advocated by Dr Millicent Danker, based on her Doctoral thesis on corporate governance (Henley Business School, 2011). In it she argues that aggressive individualism is not a sustainable basis for companies needing to deliver social and economic value, as well as building symbiotic relationships with stakeholders in an interdependent and interconnected world.

She was the inspiration for this book, which she asked me to co-author, based on our combined experience of business relationships, politics and media/public opinion. She and I had been colleagues for many years, as consultants, trainers and latterly as students, collaborating in Asia and Europe.

Despite a long-term illness, Millicent was determined we should write this book together. Sadly, this was not to be, as she died all too suddenly and prematurely at the age of 63 in the early stages of the project. Her professionalism and passion, integrity and determination were her hallmarks. Hopefully they will live on in the pages of this book and any debate it inspires.

Fortunately my colleague Dr Reginald Watts, with whom I have collaborated before, agreed to keep the flag flying in support of what Millicent so clearly articulated. I am indebted to him for jumping on board with the aircraft already on the runway.

We both have many years experience of business and politics. But being neither lawyers nor economists, (although we have dealt with enough of them), this is not a dry treatise on corporate governance reforms nor the laws of economics.

Rather it is an attempt to look at the stakeholder concept (doing well for stakeholders is good for business and society) through a variety of prisms. We try to contextualise it and by so doing join a few dots – such as West and East, reputation and responsibility, global/local, character and culture, dialogue and diplomacy and not least shareholder/stakeholder.

An over concentration on shareholder value, which some believe led to the many scandals of recent years, will be under even greater scrutiny. It is not understood, let alone accepted in many parts of the world. What is required is leadership by heads of private companies, as well as others interested in the role of business, putting the case for business in society, human capitalism, that balances shareholder with stakeholder primacy.

We have tried to reflect Millicent's high ideals in everything we wrote and hope, as she intended, that it will be a worthy contribution to an important debate in countries, cities, boardrooms, offices, parliaments universities, public squares and not forgetting internet chatrooms around the world.

This book is Millicent Danker's legacy. Reginald and I hope we have lived up to her expectations.

Dr Roger Hayes

Foreword

In 1970 Milton Friedman famously declared that the only objective of business was to maximise profits for its shareholders. For a while, such a one-dimensional view of corporate purpose was an influential and widely quoted perspective. But by the 2000s it had become largely discredited. Such a simplistic vision of company motivation offers little to business leaders who aspire to create respected enterprises and ensure long-term economic viability.

In 2009, Jack Welch – the former CEO of General Electric and one of the world's most admired business figures – was ready to admit that 'shareholder value is the dumbest idea in the world. Shareholder value is a result, not a strategy … your main constituencies are your employees, your customers and your products'. More recently, Jack Ma – the founder of Internet giant Alibaba – has warned potential investors that his business will always put customers first, employees second and shareholders third. Far from deterring investors, Alibaba's 2014 listing on the New York Stock Exchange (the largest initial public offering in history) was a roaring success.

This book builds on the insight that societal expectations about business are changing. We are living in a world in which global communications are magnifying the scrutiny to which corporations are subjected. Social awareness of a range of previously opaque business issues – from executive pay to respect for human rights along the supply chain – is growing. Society expects companies to act as 'good corporate citizens'. It is no longer acceptable for business to see itself as an entirely private matter for company managers, directors and shareholders – wider society demands that the enterprises in its midst are doing the right thing.

However, the relationship between some parts of business and society is currently at a low ebb. The experience of the financial crisis and other corporate scandals has reinforced public scepticism of the behaviour and motives of big corporations. That is why this book's notion of the collaborative enterprise – which engages and partners with a wide range of stakeholders on the basis of strong ethical principles – is such a powerful prescription for the future.

The issue of trust is central to the position of business in society. The extent to which a business and its leaders are trusted will be based on numerous factors including a reputation for honesty and integrity, transparency and good communication, and a track record of translating fine intentions into concrete actions.

This book provides business leaders with guidance and inspiration on how to nurture a culture which can help build trust in business. Although the journey is far from easy, it offers organisations a roadmap that, if applied with rigour and sincerity, can help put business back where it should be – as the respected champion of wealth creation and social progress which attracts the brightest and the best.

Dr Roger Barker
Director of Corporate Governance and Professional Standards,
Institute of Directors

PART I
Meeting the Global Challenge:
A Collaborative Paradigm

MEETING THE GLOBAL CHALLENGE

A Collaborative Paradigm

INTRODUCTION and CHAPTER 1

CHAPTERS 2 and 3

Redefining the Purpose of Business

Corporate Responsibility – Ethics   The Dialogue of Diplomacy

ARE YOU READY?

CHAPTERS 4, 5 and 6

Resolving the Stakeholder/Shareholder Conflict   Longer Term Business Focus

Reputation in Relationships   Societal Change and Urbanisation

The Leadership Challenge   Nano T- Women and Work, Digital Millennials

CHAPTERS 7 and 8

and PAST IS PROLOGUE

Reinventing Business Studies

The Collaborative Ties That Bind: A Network of Shared Values

Introduction

In an uncertain and complex world leaders should not merely respond to the speed of change but attempt to anticipate change. Sometimes it is unexpected, sometimes the signs are there, but the dots are not joined together. Many senior executives are disconnected from the environment around them – too busy, too focused, too inward looking, developing strategies based on past experience. More usually leaders blunder on trying to continue as before in the hope that things will soon be back to normal. Couple the collusion of global forces with the convergence of economics, politics and culture, there is no normal. The *new* normal must be navigated, negotiated, networked and a narrative built around it. There will be as much collaboration as competition, a greater need to listen, learn, link and lead. Are you ready?

Change is multi-faceted and if, for example, the economy swings back, social change has moved on, with digital communications taking up the slack or pressure groups becoming more demanding, invalidating existing operating models. Customers are also citizens. Some shareholders take a long-term view. Economists worry about capital markets, but ignore social disruptions. Non-Governmental Organisations (NGOs) have negative visions of capitalism and Internet geeks argue for a world united by the Web. In 'A Future Perfect: The Challenge and Hidden Promise of Globalisation' (2000) Mickelthwait and Wooldridge wrote: 'Business people often know the meat and bones of the subject (of globalisation) better than anyone else does – the companies and products that are drawing the world together – but they are too wrapped up in the struggle for profits to consider the wider picture.' Future leaders will need multidimensional thinking, operating in multiple timeframes, and the ability to connect unconnected disciplines and be prepared for continuous learning.

In the new era, centres of economic activity will shift dramatically, not just globally, but regionally. The consumer landscapes in India, China, Brazil and Africa are expanding significantly, with massive cultural implications. Technological change has become a cliché, but equally important is behaviour changing, people forming relationships in ways unforeseen. Cities will become as important as countries, forming new kinds of communities, not just Mumbai, Dubai and Shanghai, according to McKinsey & Co.,(2013/14) but Porto Allegro,

Brazil, Kumasi, Ghana and Tianjin, China. Snippets of information, often hidden in social media streams, offer leaders a valuable new tool for staying ahead, so long as senior leaders are sensitive to these 'weak signals'.

The role of business will come under even more scrutiny as will that of government. Both need to adapt to a changing ecosystem in which the biggest challenges cross the boundaries of the public, private and non-profit sectors, requiring much closer collaboration. Just as governments have an opportunity to figure out how all stakeholders should work together on an issue or in a sector, so too do corporations need to move beyond narrow self-interest and short-termism to balance stakeholder expectations. In large and unequal newly emerging economic powerhouses like Brazil, India and Indonesia, the forms of capitalism that privilege private wealth creation and shareholder value above all, are ultimately incompatible with democratic politics. The growing level of concentration of capital experienced now in the more advanced countries where the middle classes are being squeezed is unsustainable and could eventually lead to a political backlash. The level of house prices in Singapore and London are classic examples of tension. The smarter enterprise has the potential to create sustainable economic and societal growth. But this will require new ways of working, new mind-sets.

The purpose of the book therefore is to identify and join up the signals of change in an interdependent, interconnected and intercultural world, define what qualities will be needed by heads of organisations in business, government, global charities or within the tidal wave of NGOs strewn across the world and establish a model, particularly for business organisations and the higher education system that feeds them. The tool-kit is there ready to be unpacked. The only question is whether ambitious managers aiming for the sky are sensitive enough to read those signals and develop the ambidextrous skills to lead so as to help create a collaborative paradigm within and between organisations and the global system.

The collaborative paradigm requires of business and other leaders an understanding of:

1.   The convergence of business, government, civil society/ public opinion.

2.   The interdependence of the global environment, countries, cities and communities.

3.   Balancing self with societal interest.

4.   Understanding the link between rational and emotional.

5.   Adopting an interdisciplinary approach to concepts and fields of study.

6.   Eroding barriers between countries, institutions and departments.

7.   The interaction of theory and practice.

8.   Co-creating and engaging with, often uncomfortable stakeholders.

9.   Being critical of overly 'Western-centric' interpretations, including short-termism.

10.   Replacing a command and control mentality with one of conversation and collaboration.

As former United Nations (UN) Secretary–General Dag Hammarskjold was fond of saying – setting the bar higher than was thought possible, then having scaled it, realising it was too low.

Chapter 1

'Google Glasses': Reframing the Leadership Landscape

Different chapters serve to deliver goods to various destinations with diverse outcomes, attempting to attract different stakeholder communities to the central theme of leading for stakeholder value via a collaborative paradigm, a relational approach, creating value together. The relationship is the last driver of sustainable value. To identify the key issues and develop the trust to build coalitions and form partnerships means building relationships, requiring dialogue and diplomacy skills that will be picked apart later in the book. This chapter discusses not just global challenges but also opportunities, which can help governments, corporations and other institutions distinguish themselves and their organisations. The conditions are that the world has been turned upside down. The context is one of no place to hide, combined with a decline of deference with less trust in institutions and their leaders than ever before. The consequences are momentous for business, government and civil society whether in the emerging world or the traditional, advanced economies. To be sustainable means combining economic with social value. This in turn demands a stakeholder approach predicated on the emergence of new kinds of leaders. It is safe to assume that what got us here won't get us there. Einstein was right when observing that you can't solve a problem with the same mind-set that created it. Whereas financial capital supported physical capital in earlier ages, in a globalised world characterised by interconnectedness and interdependence, change and complexity, social capital has become vital currency. Such capital requires networking, negotiating, navigation and narrative skills as never before and a completely new mind-set.

Countries, corporations and civil society are converged. Singapore is a city as well as a state, largely comprising multinational corporations. Companies are competing against countries, often via their sovereign wealth funds. The European Union (EU) is a 'network' of states, London is effectively a city–state economically distinct from the United Kingdom (UK). Mayors from China to the United States (US) are working with business from the ground up, not top-down, involving local individuals and organisations, and in the process forming new kinds of communities. We are living with informational capitalism and strong profit seeking, often at the cost of soul searching. This is much needed when, despite the growth of middle classes from China to India, poverty and social exclusion lurk not far away, or in the case of Rio de Janeiro and Mumbai, right next door. Living in a global neighbourhood, these issues are everyone's business. It is not a question of the state versus the free-market, but closer collaboration between business, government and civil societies in creating and maintaining communities. To achieve those will require far greater business and broader leadership. But what are the essential elements leaders need and the context – cultural, political and economic – within which it operates? This book will attempt to provide an answer to that question.

The Diffusion of Power

Globalisation and the information, communications and telecommunications revolution has gone to a whole new level, from connected to hyper-connected. Tom Friedman (2005), the *New York Times* columnist, who coined the term 'flat' to describe the shape of the new world believes this means we all have to study harder, work smarter and adapt quicker than ever before. So yes – we have to learn to manage complexity and deal with connected capitalism by creating smarter enterprises. What's more, this same phenomenon enables the 'globalisation of anger', super-empowering individuals to challenge hierarchies and traditional authority figures as never before, from government and business to science and religion. This phenomenon is making governing, managing and influencing harder, hence the need for a new kind of leadership. Effectively the pyramid of power has been turned upside down. As CNN's Fareed Zakaria (2008) put it: 'Power is shifting away from nation states up, down and sideways.' More and more 'actors', starting with environmental NGOs and, more recently, multinational corporations, 24/7 TV news and now 'citizen journalists' and 'civil society activists', are taking to the global political stage. Anand Mahindra, Chairman of Mahindra Group, noted the 28 elected States of India (some larger than many countries) and the new cities created will be catalysts for India's growth, emanating from an urban middle class whose interests transcend culture. This could enable India to pick up the slack from a slowing China. Michael Bloomberg, former Mayor of New York, argues that because cities are closest to the majority of the world's people, they are better able than nations to get things fixed. London's Mayor, Boris Johnson, would no doubt echo that sentiment.

We know that power is shifting from West to East, hierarchical organisations to lateral ones, even from dictatorships to protest movements. As Moises Naim, former journalist and Venezuelan Minister wrote (2013): 'Power is easier to get, harder to use and easier to lose ... the decay of power is changing the world'. Previous Heads of State and chief executive officers (CEOs) of large corporations, not to mention other institutions such as the Catholic Church, dealt with fewer challenges, competitors and constraints, such as media scrutiny, global cultural clashes and citizen activism than is the case these days. A photograph of Charles de Gaulle surrounded by his officials while commanding their absolute attention serves as a metaphor for an old style of leadership that no longer works. Compared to a Churchill, the status and credibility of Prime Ministers today is much diminished. Part of the reason must be over-exposure, but one of the keys then was they had experience of battle. Steve Jobs partly became a leader because he had actually designed the first Apple computer in his garage. New York Mayor Rudy Giuliani became a leadership role model because he had led New York so effectively at a challenging moment. As the British monarchy has found over recent years, the mystique has been lost, with barriers to entry falling. So Prime Ministers and CEOs now have to compete with celebrities and dissidents for attention, not to mention mayors.

Despite the different reasons behind recent protests, violent clashes from Russia to Turkey, Brazil to Egypt, Hong Kong to Malaysia, Bahrain to India, Greece to Spain – just as in 1848, 1968 and 1989 when people also found 'a collective voice' – they have much in common. It is interesting that protests have been as active in democracies as dictatorships – that it is largely ordinary, middle-class people condemning the alleged corruption, inefficiency and arrogance of the 'folks' in charge, or in some instances simply the alienation and detachment from the centre, recently observed in the UK, France and Spain. The Turkish Prime Minister even explicitly blamed 'a menace called Twitter' for the June 2013 Istanbul riots and has tried to ban all social media; a bit like trying to contain a breached dam. If it is now harder to govern, it is easier to refuse to be governed. Even in dictatorships we consent to be ruled. The reason is that the fear has gone, because we are not alone. A concern is that some media spreads information so fast that the organisational core becomes swamped and the agenda blurred. This makes it difficult to resolve conflict. Yet as unemployment and inequalities soar and the emerging world witnesses the political expectations of a rapidly growing middle class, it has become even more important for political, business and civil society leaders to anticipate and reconcile some of these conflicting interests.

Where are the Leaders?

Yet, just at a time when heads of institutions should be at the top of their game, they are falling short. In the UK, when traditional politics was becoming corroded by the reasons and results of the Iraq war and citizens were seeking alternative voices, where were the leaders of civil society, such as The Church of England? They were locked in internal squabbles, communicating in a manner more akin to a monastery than a public square. (At least the relatively new Archbishop of Canterbury, Justin Welby, combining a business and political background, has called for 'a revolution' in his church.)

Erik Schmidt of Google fame has argued that revolutions are easier to start than finish, with greater connectivity involving the young. This leads to more protests, full regime change or reform hampered by 'a lack of sustainable leaders and savvier state responses'. Sometimes, as in the case of the 2011 London riots sparked by a police killing, the results were marked by lawlessness. The Occupy Movement, which protested in Sydney, London and New York against income disparities between bankers and ordinary people were more restrained in their protests by camping outside symbolic buildings. UK Uncut, however, raised the issue of tax avoidance among multinational corporations such as Vodafone and Starbucks. This led to politicians taking up this issue as a legitimate grievance, resulting in a grilling in parliament of their hapless executives. The Chairman of Christian Aid spoke out that financial secrecy works against human dignity, so multinational corporations should pay proper taxes in less-developed countries where they operate. This is a good example of the interconnectedness being discussed in this book and the interdependence between business, politics and public opinion. The tragic ferry disaster in South Korea and the disappearance of the Malaysian aircraft in 2014 are other examples of organisational and human-siloed thinking.

Convergence

Just as power has become more diffuse, so too, according to Mickelthwait and Wooldridge (2000), has 'the internet fused media, politics and economics to the point where it is impossible to change one of these areas without impacting the other'.

Trade trumps missiles in today's global power plays with traditional international politics being overtaken by economic diplomacy. This refers to the changing balance between the advanced and rising states in various trade negotiations and the risk of competing blocs, rather than open global arrangements. Following a decade of rapid growth, large swathes of Africa are going digital, particularly the cities. There are more African democracies than hitherto. Yet poverty remains stubbornly high. In South Africa, a first world economy lives next door to grinding poverty, which a broader capitalism collaborating with government and civil society could do much to avert. This is thanks to significant infrastructure investment, combined with low-cost smart phones and tablets enabling millions to connect. It will have a major impact on governance, agriculture, retail, health-care, education and financial services.

Creating Shared Value

So where might the future with its never-before-seen challenges and opportunities take us? Ericsson, a Swedish high-tech firm, believes in sharing knowledge about the future: 'If we do, the future might not be a place we are going, but a place we create' (Ericsson, 2013). Vincent Cerf, Chief Internet evangelist at Google and father of the Internet, sees computers becoming even more intelligent, with mobile phone 'our companions rather than simply a device' (Ericsson, 2013). Yet changes in the climate and unsustainable pollution in China does mean the world could follow the way of the Roman and Mayan civilisations, by simply collapsing. Technology will help, but leadership matters more and leadership at different levels. Technology may have been a catalyst that brought down the Soviet Union but, with political power more diffuse, politicians should perhaps be humble and open minded. The same could be said for business leaders, not to mention media pundits.

Futurologist, Anne Lise Kjaer, argues (EUROSME Conference, 2013) that because only one in five company or product brands are perceived to make any meaningful difference to peoples' lives, institutions must begin to explore how to deliver 'real' value to communities. The Samso Energy Academy in Denmark demonstrates how decentralised collaboration, innovation and empowerment are key components of citizen participation. These are bonded by 'authentic story-telling'. Sandra Macleod, CEO of Mindful Reputation, sums it up thus: 'As risk becomes more complex, transparency more radical and reputation more dear with trust as the prize, through better alignment with stakeholder values and expectations, attention to authentic reputation creates very real value' (2014). Whereas, in a rational context, Kjaer maintains, the key values are diversity and dialogue, in an emotional one, community and engagement values should be added. She talks about the era of 'meaningful consumption', promoting 'radical openness' as key to the digital reputation economy.

She refers to her home country Denmark as having the lowest corruption in the world due to its transparent system of E-Government. There is a need for sharing, mobility and affinity, aided by 'big data networks'. Social capital and shared values are the drivers of global economic clusters. In a hyper-connected society, social trends have the ability to reach further and move faster with grassroots concerns reaching a global audience. To create a 'multi-dimensional' future will require left-brain facts and analysis together with right-brain bigger picture, conceptual thinking, Kjaer asserts. The twentieth-century left-brain outlook driven by ego, power, status and wealth is obsolete and should be replaced by caring, community and the environment. Companies will win if they are able to manage the data deluge and complexity while also connecting with people for the purpose of inspiring and enriching their lives. The information revolution is replacing one kind of management (command and control) with another (self-organising networks), to create societal as well as economic value. This is now part of *how* business should be done.

It is no accident that Pope Francis in his first 'Apostolic Exhortation' wrote of the need for 'an inclusive and compassionate church' to offset the 'globalisation of indifference'. Since then he has demonstrated this in various ways.

The End of History?

Thus, while we may not have reached 'The End of History' as Francis Fukuyama predicted in 1990, symbolised by the fall of the Berlin Wall, with many different shades of government and hues of capitalism being practised, the world has arguably reached a 'critical juncture'. In summary, as a result of 'ideas on the rise' and 'a bad mood rising', the ever more sophisticated consumer/citizen determines the 'licence to operate'. We live in a stakeholder-centric world!

The growth of more powerful stakeholders has hit business. Now a simple count of the global top 500 companies that did not exist ten years ago shows how relative newcomers are replacing them. In the second half of 2010, the midst of the economic recession, the top ten hedge funds (most unknown names) earned more than the worlds' largest banks combined. The world's largest steel company Arcelor-Mittal has Indian origins and Budweiser is now owned by the world's largest beer company, a Brazilian company. The world's richest man is a Mexican business magnate. More and more of the world's largest companies have headquarters in China, India, South Korea, Brazil and the Gulf. Corporate dominance is under siege. Corporations are increasingly vulnerable to reputation disasters affecting their brands. BP and News Corporation spring to mind. Kodak's demise illustrates that leadership is not what it used to be. Another indicator is that more and more CEOs are leaving their posts sooner than before and their companies suffering reputation dents earlier than before.

New Kinds of Leaders

While globalisation and the Internet have played a role, a more fundamental explanation of power diffusion is, explains Moises Naim (2013), a combination of *more* of everything, *mobility* of people, goods, capital and *mentality* – changes in expectations, mind-sets and aspirations. All these were witnessed in the Arab and other Springs. But just as concentration of power causes problems, so too does diffusion cause paralysis – witness gridlock in Washington DC. There is a paradox here that just as corporations have more political influence and geographic spread than before, they have never been more exposed. Their wings having been clipped, although the same holds true for governments, trade unions, foundations and religious organisations. As global problems multiply and issues become more complex, the capacity of governments to reach agreement and collaborate with civil society and business is diminishing. This is a result of failure of leadership, predicated on seeing the bigger picture, taking a longer-term view, listening to others and trusting others to bring solutions. What is needed is to endow our leaders across sectors and cultures with the capacity to contain 'the decay of power', while creating new mechanisms of global governance.

The global public space is both a challenge and an opportunity. With the boundaries between institutions blurred and between countries eroded, public or private sector leaders thrust into the global spotlight require a broader range of skills, new methodologies and a fresh mind-set. This book is an attempt to define and elaborate what these are.

Above all this has implications for those who seek to lead these organisations and who have responsibility towards that broader ecosystem of stakeholders. Stakeholders who are sometimes alien are often uncomfortable, yet all need nurturing and engagement. In fact the state is increasingly becoming a 'strategic enabler', collaborating with a whole network of stakeholders on issues such as climate change or the eradication of diseases. On the other hand, the corporation is becoming more human, concerned with broader societal issues, in some instances fulfilling the role of the state. For instance, sometimes it provides public services such as schools and hospitals, building roads and ensuring clean water. One of the fastest growth areas in places such as Africa and India is collaboration between government, private companies and NGOs in the area of water diplomacy. The Edelman Trust Barometer (2013) calls this 'mutual social responsibility' based around engagement and integrity. The obsession with profit motive to the exclusion of all else is the biggest obstacle to trust. Hence the narrative needs to change.

Tomorrow's global company needs to redefine success in terms of positive impacts, not just for business but also society, where vision and values are aligned and institutions collaborate as well as compete. This is what Shell means by 'Profits, People and Planet' and PepsiCo calls 'Performance with Purpose'. World affairs is now less about official business between states and more about managing the effects of globalisation, integration, political uncertainty and cultural divides. Indeed, lack of sensitivity to culture may well limit public policy options, just as business must embrace public sentiment. This demands they be instruments of social change. New media provides opportunities for co-creation, conversations and myriad connections. This means it is no longer always about 'me'. These forces are forging a convergence of institutions and approaches to global governance (not the same as global government), while culture is the prism through which many view international affairs.

What governments and companies need today is 'collaborative diplomacy', where hard power is replaced by psychological authority and the modern executive can demonstrate 'inspirational' leadership. However, just as national governments are expected by their citizens to solve problems requiring international solutions, (take, for instance, Singapore and Malaysia regularly suffering from the haze caused by illegal logging in neighbouring Indonesia), so too are corporations 'between a rock and a hard place'. On the one hand they are under relentless pressure to compete and perform, on the other they are expected to deploy their financial and human capacity on broader social issues.

So what does leadership in this demanding context imply? It is about good governance, integrity and responsible behaviour, reflected in building sustainable relationships with stakeholders.

Collaboration and culture are concepts that in a more connected, conversational, transparent and less trusting world are proving difficult for management to get their heads around. They appear ill-equipped to face newly empowered and often multi-cultural stakeholders. Business leaders will need to engage more beyond their narrow stakeholder community of shareholders, customers and employees if they are to avoid some of the corporate scandals that have taken place in recent years. Leaders need to remain true to their own internal compass or 'True North'. Staying on message may be off radar if it is not credible in the post TV age. Leaders need to strip away the artifice, be authentic and true to themselves.

Smarter Enterprises

A poll of 250 internal communications officers in companies around the world revealed remarkable convergence of opinion that two-thirds of business leaders are failing to engage with their stakeholders, including employees. This provides a clear indication that companies are insufficiently forward-focused and ill-prepared for change. A book aptly named *The Extreme Future* (Canton, 2006) spelled out that drastic adjustments in work, community and relationships will force companies to adapt quickly to radical *changes,* all linked to *speed, complexity, risk* and *surprise.* Hence there is an urgent need to navigate, track and analyse the future. Perhaps we are witnessing the evolution of the 'smarter enterprise' that makes decisions, creates and delivers value, but in different ways. According to IBM's CEO Virginia Rometty, writing in *The Economist* The World in 2014, smarter enterprises will make decisions by capturing data and applying predictive analytics, rather than just relying on past experience. Smarter enterprises will create smarter products – from cars to crops – not simply communicating to target audiences, but having a dialogue with human beings, transforming relationships with stakeholders, which will hopefully redefine management teaching. 'The emerging smarter enterprise has the potential to be a powerful force for global economic growth and sustainable, democratic and societal progress,' writes Rometty (2014).

The old solutions no longer work and these authors are hopeful that heads of organisations in India, Brazil, Malaysia and China will leapfrog into greater thought-leadership and statesmanship by learning the lessons of the West. Perhaps they will do that by mixing the rational calculation of Max Weber's 'Protestant Ethic' with the Buddhist emphasis on 'mindfulness'. (Google offers an internal course, aptly entitled 'Search Inside Yourself'.) Maybe they will learn from the corporate scandals and reputation disasters that have plagued companies in the West. CEOs must build beyond peer-to-peer alliances (the 'old boy' network among non-executive directors), investing in new collaborations. These should reflect the rise in citizen/consumer power, the changing nature of the state and broader stakeholder legitimacy beyond the traditional shareholder primacy model.

The Global Thinkers Forum (GTF) set up in 2011 as a global platform for excellence in leadership advocates a more reflective approach on issues as diverse as global citizenship, conflict resolution, human rights, social justice, sustainable development, ethical values and cultural precepts. While the largest corporations with global reach and social impact, especially oil, gas and mining, monitor and report on these issues, most organisations fail to join the dots. There is a massive need to connect collective progress with individual corporate prosperity.

According to Elizabeth Filippouli (the founder of GTF) (2013), it is necessary that leaders are trained to successfully challenge incumbent behavioural patterns, invest in social capital and reengineer group thinking, all in ways that promote productive collaboration. International cooperation is now everyones' business. The efforts of *all* stakeholders are required to adapt the international system to our more interdependent world. No network exists that is sufficiently interdisciplinary, interactive and international to overcome the barriers to collective intelligence.

A study by BBC World's Nik Gowing (2009), highlighted how, in a moment of major, unexpected crisis, the institutions of power face a new, acute vulnerability of influence and effectiveness. This is due to what he described as exponential changes in portable, digital technology, which are redefining, broadening and fragmenting the nature of the media by a new breed of 'information doers'. These are the stakeholders that have a demanding set of expectations, rather than merely an 'audience' to whom transactional messages are sent.

Value and Values

The term 'value' contains a 'double entendre' – the creation of business value and 'values', as in ethical behaviour. Of course the two can be interconnected. Wheeler and Sillanpaa (1997) wrote: 'Enterprises run in the interests of a wide range of stakeholders are more likely to behave responsibly, thus creating two kinds of value-commercial and social.' Two decades ago, even management guru, Peter Drucker, who was alleged to have said 'the business of business is business', thought that a social problem should be transformed into an economic benefit. In the intervening years there has developed a lively debate over the role of business in society. This has veered between corporate social responsibility (CSR) as simply box ticking and siloed from the main business issues to embedding an ethical and societal approach into the DNA of the corporate culture, reflected in the products and services. Unilever is a good example of this last approach, ensuring that their products should not just be useful but mirror the meaning in peoples' lives.

As stakeholder theorists argue in the context of globalisation, the Internet and wider social and environmental developments, everyone is now having to address three interwoven concepts. These are corporate responsibility, sustainable development and a stakeholder approach to strategic management, irrespective of the legal construct of the firm. The problem is that the allocation of resources between a wider array of stakeholders is becoming more complex. Not least is this due to the need to lead beyond borders, navigate cultural diversity and adopt international governance principles. Yet leadership is lacking and leaders have been found wanting. It's a tough old world.

Paradoxically, the greater the uncertainty, pace of change and complexity of issues, the more people are seeking confidence, optimism, meaning and resilience in their leaders. Yet there seems to be a misfit with governmental and corporate structures. Some of these soft issues, which have now become hard, do not come naturally to many. Governments are finding it difficult to govern and companies are finding it increasingly hard to balance the sometimes conflicting needs and expectations of stakeholders. After all its experience dealing with tough environments all over the world, why was BP seemingly so unprepared when forced to deal with local stakeholders after the Gulf of Mexico disaster? BP is not the only culprit.

One of the problems with the concept of leadership is that each of us thinks differently about it. We each have our own role models, usually political leaders at times of crisis, such as Gandhi, Churchill or Mandela. It differs from culture to culture and there are leaders in all walks of life and at all levels. Above all we need leaders who lead with purpose, integrity and insight, who can relate to all stakeholders. There are more than 100 different definitions with thousands of books available on the topic. There are debates around whether it is a trait or a quality, a natural or acquired ability, a skill or a competence and what leaders do as well as say.

Contextual Intelligence

Harvard Professor Joe Nye (2008), who coined the phrase 'soft power', (the power of attraction as opposed to hard military power), distinguishes between transformational and transactional leadership. In the former instance the situation calls for technical and routine solutions, in the latter adaptive change to shape events, which may take a little longer. Above all, Nye suggests, leaders need 'contextual intelligence', connecting seemingly unconnected thoughts. Some situations call for autocratic decisions and some require the opposite. Leaders must understand culture, corporate and societal, the distribution of power, followers' needs and information flows. GE Corporation prides itself on producing leaders, but many of its high fliers who moved to other companies failed to transfer their skills. There are many examples of business leaders failing at politics and vice versa. Dwight Eisenhower, however, was successful at both, Nye contends, due to contextual intelligence. Two skills are particularly important for the 'soft power' part of the mix, visionary communications and Emotional Intelligence (EQ), whereas the two hard power skills remain organisational and political. 'The vision thing' is a way of giving meaning to an idea that inspires others and is often rooted in what followers basically need or believe.

All leaders need high IQs, but as Daniel Goleman in his book *Emotional Intelligence* (1995) asserted, EQ is equally important, particularly these days. It is characterised by empathy, social skills, self-awareness, self-regulation and motivation. Because these elements have traditionally been considered 'soft', they are not usually covered in traditional training programmes. Of course high academic performance and the right technical skills remain important ingredients, but employers are gradually seeking top graduates with EQ or 'soft skills'. These comprise teamwork, clear communications, adapting well to change, smooth interactions with a wide variety of people and solving problems under pressure. Without sensitivity to the needs of others, pure cognitive intelligence and experience will be necessary but insufficient going forward.

Ronald Reagan had relatively low cognitive intelligence, but high contextual intelligence; Jimmy Carter the opposite. It is argued that George W. Bush should have shown more transactional leadership when dealing with Iraq and its aftermath, rather than the more transformative 'shock and awe' of his initial use of hard power. Devoid of contextual intelligence, being a decider is sometimes not enough. Former British Prime Minister Tony Blair has considerable ability in the articulation of vision department, but critics thought he lacked attention to detail in implementation during his time at the top. Martin Luther King learned from an immersion in an African American church how to be an inspirational leader. Bill Clinton has a sense of theatre, combined with an ability to tell stories, which sets him apart. For Gandhi it was the symbolism of his simple dress and accompanying lifestyle which told the story. Richard Branson, the British entrepreneur, often exemplified as a business leader, became a success partly as a result of brilliant public events and stunts to promote his Virgin brands. It was he who organised a business leaders' 'open letter' to governments urging them to use diplomacy to stop the violence in Ukraine during 2014. Sometimes it is as simple as walking the talk. Prime Minister Lee Hsien Loong of Singapore set the right example in 2007 when his government raised official salaries by foregoing his.

In a stakeholder context, a successful vision has to attract a variety of stakeholders, which requires listening to them. Their story is now your story. Malaysia's Minister of Information was dismissed after telling an interviewer on Al Jazeera TV news that rioters were provoking the police, while simultaneous pictures showed police using water cannons against innocent bystanders. He wasn't listening, rather propagandising. In a real-time, visual world this is no longer credible.

Capitalism, Curse or Cure?

There are some signs that capitalism is beginning to listen. The high-tech, globalised capitalism of today is very different from the post Second World War version that worked for the middle classes of the Western world, yet finds them squeezed today. The State of Delaware has set up what is called 'The B-Corp', or Benefit Corporation. These are companies charged both with earning profits for shareholders and also protecting employees or safeguarding the environment. In the old days companies put back into their local communities, but in today's virtual economy those personal constraints are eroding to the point where new structures are appropriate. The world's biggest problem is not how to make more stuff (even while it can always be better distributed), rather to achieve a more harmonious balance between short and longer-term profits. This requires social innovation, which the Occupy Movement flagged up. The trend is also being underpinned by a new generation of idealistic consumers and employees. Trader Joes in the US have unusually 'generous' salaries and health benefits for their employees, an example of short-term cost in favour of long-term benefit to the individuals, the organisation and community.

Stakeholder Theory Meets Corporate Practice

What is needed is the input of greater human consciousness – social, environmental and economic – which contains an emotional element, what has been referred to as a 'new global equity culture'. This requires a more authentic kind of leadership which reaches out to more stakeholders, many asking is the corporation sustainable? This conversation will become louder as time goes on, more focused on particular company behaviour in specific sectors. Oil and gas used to be the bogeyman, now it is financial services and, in the UK at least, utility companies. Yet it is business, more so than governments, that are ideally positioned to make the world a better place, of course working together with governments and civil society. (It is well known that half of the 100 largest economies are companies not nations and that 40 per cent of world trade is conducted via them.)

Toyota wove key social and energy concerns into the creation of the Prius hybrid car. As such the rise of social branding is an emerging role for business, particularly as consumers and communities are seeking meaning from products and company HQs, sponsorship and community activities, according to brand guru Michael Watras (2014). The problem is that many have been looking at momentous changes since 1989 through an old prism, largely dividing up the roles of government and business. Whereas, in fact, the answer resides in collaboration between a whole raft of stakeholders. For example, patients are now co-creating drugs with industry, tailored to their needs.

Now the emphasis is not only on what consumers want but what the world needs, particularly when viewed in the context of climate change, water shortages, poverty, epidemics like SARS, Ebola and not least terrorism. 'Social response capitalism' should be bridging the gap between simplistic environmental activism and pure free-market capitalism.

CSR, which grew out of the environmental movement of the 1970s and 80s, has constantly adapted to conform to governmental regulation. But usually it has not been built into the total supply chain. Leaders should articulate a vision around these challenges and opportunities, while steering the corporation in a way that reflects the convergence between global economic development, resource tensions, demographic shifts and political protests. This means knowing when to play by the rules and when to change the game. In all these authors' experience of CEOs articulating the vision and backing up with competent, clear, coherent communications, credibility is the key to leadership. Here IQ is necessary but not sufficient. Using a diplomatic metaphor, it is really a combination of stagecraft and statecraft leading to statesmanship. Nelson Mandela wearing the rugby jersey to signify reconciliation between the races at a key moment in South Africa's transformation is a classic example of the former kind of initiative in a sports diplomacy context.

Collaborative Diplomacy

A former adviser to the British Foreign Office, Lucien Hudson, wrote a paper entitled 'Leading and Supporting Strategic Collaborations' (2008), urging collaboration between government, the private sector and NGOs. The third sector needs to become more business focused, demonstrating that they can give the best return on investment in areas where they better understand public needs. The best NGOs already do this. Collaboration provides the transitional space for innovation to flourish. Hudson's model is based on a spectrum ranging from conflict (win–lose) to collaboration (win–win), with negotiation in between. Collaboration is about assertion and cooperation, with roles and boundaries constantly being renegotiated. However, what is so often lacking is the right spirit on both sides. Hudson wrote: 'What holds us back is not the technology, but the culture and behaviour that goes with collaboration' (2008). This is an advanced form of leadership.

Warren Bennis (2003), the management author, has argued that among the disciplines critical to modern leadership are those related to communications because, as the diplomatic metaphor alludes, it is partly a performance art. Leaders need a compelling narrative they are able to share with their followers using rhetoric as part of the equation. Queen Elizabeth I once remarked: 'We princes are set on stages in sight and view of all the world.' Another factor is that public leaders often interact with their followers filtered through the media, especially now with new media so pervasive. This is certainly the case with consumers and employees. Political leaders in the Arab world have learned too late that leadership requires a variety of voices and techniques. How are business leaders differently perceived if they appear in the news as opposed to op-ed pages or on a TV talk show rather than a blog? It should be noted that a stakeholder environment of leadership calls for the ability to mobilise others as collaborators. In this environment stakeholders join rather than simply follow the leader.

Authenticity Root Construct

The study of leadership is in its early stages but there is an emerging consensus, according to leading theorist Bruce Avolio (Avolio and Gardner, 2005), that the notion of 'authenticity' is a root construct of leadership. This becomes all the more so as collaboration between institutions is more necessary and there is a greater need to engage with stakeholders, many of whom define themselves and some of whom make uncomfortable bedfellows. Jack Welch, former GE

Chairman, put it this way: 'You're a leader now. It's not about you anymore. It's about them' (2005). Incidentally Welch believes 'candour' to be one of the defining characteristics of effective leaders, providing regular feedback to colleagues. This is akin to a star tennis player being mentored by his coach.

For all these reasons 'leading for stakeholder value' is vital going forward. Corporations are not called 'human institutions' for nothing. There is a growing awareness that some of the world's most pressing problems need cross-sectional efforts and collaboration between government, NGOs and corporations. No one institution can solve them alone. Spanning sectors and bridging boundaries is not easy, as multiple vested interests have to be squared in this flatter world, attempting to build a sustainable future.

Cosmopolitan Leaders

Companies can no longer simply comply, merely concentrating on maximising shareholder value. Business leaders are expected to do more, yet they are less trusted. The demise of the global financial sector in terms of trust is a case in point. In light of rising expectations, yet declining legitimacy, a new cadre of 'cosmopolitan' leaders should emerge. Their role would be to create a principle-driven global community seeking to build human capabilities. The stakeholder model has proved useful in this regard. Yet business leaders in fairness are faced with multiple claims, based on often conflicting values. Responsible leaders therefore need to reconcile these competing claims by engaging in an array of relationships beyond their close entourage. Hence the emphasis is on dialogue and diplomacy. Responsible global leaders ensure that all stakeholders are recognised and that a participative dialogue occurs. This is called 'weaving a web of sustainable relationships'. Corporations have relative power, privilege and potential to achieve great things in the world, but only if they become smarter, collaborative enterprises.

Many corporations have adopted what Elkington, in the book *Cannibals With Forks* (1997), described as 'the triple bottom-line' approach, balancing global stakeholder claims, particularly as the centre of gravity shifts East and South, creating new social and humanitarian challenges. The integration of value creation transcends national boundaries, impeding the ability of the nation state to moderate the outcomes of the economic, social and political systems. This leads inexorably to governance gaps. With the public interest insufficiently served, business must in certain instances play a greater political role.

This is why corporate diplomacy has become so important a skill and mind-set for CEOs and their advisers.

Indra Nooyi, CEO of PepsiCo (at a diplomatic seminar in Delhi in 2010), expressed the view that just as the diplomat spends some of the time as a travelling salesperson extolling the virtues of a country's products and services to the temporary host country, so too do CEOs add political and social leadership to their repertoire. Muhammad Yunus, the microfinance pioneer, once said: 'We create what we want. What we want and how we get it depends on our mind-sets as business leaders and citizens of the world.'

We haven't yet arrived at the global civic ethic shared by all stakeholders, let alone embodied this in an evolving system of international norms such as propounded by the Commission on Global Governance. Yet the collective power of people to shape the future is greater now than ever before and the need to exercise it more compelling if our world is to become secure and sustainable. The world is certainly watching. Stakeholders are demanding transparency, with some acutely attuned to every facet of the business, from local community outreach to the supply chain. According to the Reputation Institute's 2013 survey, it is among those companies where the CEO has managed to stay in place for a decade or so that reputation is taken more seriously. There are barriers to progress when the organisation is siloed. Reputation needs to involve the entire organisation, becoming part of the corporate culture as well as being a crucial component of the CEO's job spec.

The survey revealed the main challenges to be lack of a structured process for integrating reputation into business management, and failure to leverage knowledge to make it relevant across all stakeholders and research, which is not comparable. The role of reputation in delivering business value is greater for brands seeking to transition into emerging markets, where consumerism is changing rapidly and there is a close link between national development and economic growth. The growing role of the East only serves to remind many in the West how many Asian cultures are built on the importance of relationships and the value placed on trust and reciprocity. It's all related to culture, another link to the concept of diplomacy.

For Huawei, the world's number two telecommunications manufacturer, the challenge is to spell out that it is a global organisation rather than related to a particular country (China). As a result of security concerns raised in the West, the company has recently begun to explain and position itself in a new way, ushering in an era of transparency consistent with its global growth.

Although, while some businesses view themselves as stateless, the national symbolism for a German car company is quite helpful. It is significant that, unlike the management ideas that emanated from Japanese manufacturing companies in the 1970s and 80s, companies like Huawei are good at learning and applying techniques already tested in the West. The company is also experimenting with a rotating CEOs concept, a new idea in governance.

Trade conflicts and mistrust of competitors are nothing new, but the new era of Asian investment in the markets of the West requires a political will and the emergence of trust between the worlds' business partners, accompanied by a new kind of leadership. CEOs will need to understand culture and geopolitics like never before, just as diplomats are having to understand communications and business strategy/marketing. But if the East is ready for the journey, is the West ready to receive Asian business as trading partners and potentially owners? The biggest two investors in London are Chinese. These are areas of public diplomacy that companies and governments need to be sensitive to, especially when some nation brands are perceived as threats.

Significantly, The McKinsey Quarterly review (2014) of Chinese business leadership referred to a need for leaders to devote particular attention to people issues, teamwork, communications, presentation skills and culture. Another skill will be the ability to read the external environment and build a network that intersects with government, business and civil society. This is important, whether inside China or in places such as Africa, where Chinese companies are building roads and hospitals while simultaneously extracting oil and minerals.

Managing conflict and dispelling cultural, political and regulatory differences will remain a tough task for Asian corporations as they develop links in the more sophisticated and more transparent West. Concerns have already been raised about Chinese intentions in Africa. Cross-border investments are difficult due to cultural differences, expectations, language barriers, legal and regulatory frameworks and mistrust between business and government, not to mention between governments. With much of the Asian and Middle-East investments in the West in strategic sectors, business leaders have to tackle the notion that there is something innately geopolitical in their decision to strike out onto the global stage, rather than purely good old-fashioned economic demand and supply. Trust is the central commodity in the political and economic relationship between the superpowers and the new kids on the block.

In this new world, information about standards is more available not just to business partners and customers but also to activists. The death of 112 workers in a textile factory in Bangladesh in November 2012 producing clothing for Western retailers springs to mind. As does the building collapse in Dhaka in the same sector a few months later. As a result, Swedish clothing giant H&M (which did not produce garments there, but is the largest buyer from Bangladesh) signed a pledge to help finance fire safety and building regulation improvements there and in other factories. In that sense, the company took a stakeholder leadership role. In the digital age there is certainly no hiding place, with NGOs, activists and social media users monitoring companies. These companies should assume they are being scrutinised and act upon it. The Ethical Trading Initiative in the retail sector and the Extractive Industries Transparency Initiative in the mining sector allowing communities to share in the economic benefits of oil, gas and minerals are good examples of stakeholder collaboration.

In India, Africa and Asia local communities are key collaborators, even for smaller companies exporting and setting up operations. It is not just companies like Starbucks that are helping to create a sustainable future for communities via coffee and tea Fair Trade initiatives. British small to medium enterprises (SMEs) moving into Indian states are linking up not only with joint venture companies, but also with local communities and NGOs linked to health and education. The fatal poisoning of 23 children in July 2013 as a result of a contaminated meal shows that growth and democracy are not enough. You need good government and governance too. The children from one of India's poorest states, Bihar, however, were unusual in having a school to attend and a lunch to eat! The case for government just getting out of the way, made in 2000 by a former India chief executive of P&G, Gurcharan Das, looks a little optimistic now. What is needed is not just the invisible hand of the market, but the visible hand of effective government. Mr Modi seems intent on providing it.

As a result of all these trends, perhaps we now live in a world where less 'heroic' leadership is required, and maybe more 'reflective'. There's now more debate around team leadership and what a critical factor that is for effective organisational change.

Noted scholar Noel Tichy argued that: 'Traditional managerial skills, such as financial acumen, manufacturing expertise and marketing prowess are important ingredients in most organisational success stories, but not sufficient for organisational transformation and sustainability. The focus on the most critical element, leadership is needed as organisations are challenged by an increasingly competitive environment' (quoted in Oppel, 2007). This author would probably also add more complex and collaborative environments.

A Culture of Listening and Learning

A study on leadership qualities revealed the most important to be the creation of a more generous society worldwide and that this should be embedded in the corporate culture. Another quality is the ability to deal with uncertainty, all fuelled by the speed and impact of technology. Dealing with uncertainty demands listening and learning skills. As Starbucks is fond of saying in its promotional literature: 'We listen, learn and try to do the right thing.' Integration is a key quality highlighted in the survey, another being previous experience in international environments, which teaches empathy with other cultures. This is extremely important when working in emerging countries that are trying to manage the instability resulting from inequalities and extremes of wealth and lifestyles, sometimes cheek by jowl.

Characteristics of future global leaders will be dynamic people skills, foreign language proficiency, exposure to multi-cultural environments and multi-disciplinary perspectives.

A key follower should be the employee. Occasionally they become whistle-blowers (in the case of the Japanese company Olympus in 2011, the British CEO Michael Woodford himself!), but generally they should be the organisation's best 'ambassadors'. How many surveys do we read of the company's PR being out of alignment with customer interaction with employees? Banks are often cited. The value of employees as the company's main communication asset can never be underestimated, especially in today's social media era when employees possess numerous tools to initiate conversations about the organisation in the public domain. Insiders' views are often seen as more credible than some other stakeholders. The very public resignation of a Goldman Sachs executive director in 2012 illustrated to the corporate world why employees are a vital stakeholder, if not the most vital. It is not just external PR efforts that affect reputation, but also managements' leadership qualities, communications mind-set, competence and style operating internally. Today's employees are constantly seeking value alignment with their employer. A recent study by The Institute for Public Relations in 2013 showed that employees tend to like and respect the company more when they are led by 'authentic' leaders – transparent and true.

Amidst the various reports on the global financial crisis, corporate scandals and managerial misconduct over many years, a common denominator is attributing the failures to the challenges of global business, its increasing overlap with geopolitics, with lack of ethics a key factor.

As a consequence, theory and practice are struggling with the task of reconceptualising the role of corporations and their leaders in society, in order to address the growing ecosystem of stakeholders' surge of concerns in the international court of public opinion. For leaders this means that they should think of the consequences of their conduct for all stakeholders that could be affected – that they recognise the legitimate claims of those affected stakeholders and use their influence to initiate active stakeholder dialogues. In this sense responsible leadership is distinct from transformative leadership approaches, although the two can be mutually reinforcing. Good leadership matters. Good meaning effective and ethical.

Leaders Need Collaborators

Leadership is fast becoming a vital ingredient in success or failure. This is not leadership as it once was, but a new kind that this book will try to explore. It's a leadership that needs to be sensitive to new stakeholders and balance their expectations, a leadership adding a new set of strategic and soft skills, including communicating and collaborating in new ways. Many environmental challenges cross country or organisational boundaries, so that the best option is to collaborate – with governments, NGOs and local communities as well as other companies. Indeed, the diffusion of communication technologies and globalisation is making all forms of top-down control weaker, including autocratic. Relying on national governments alone to deliver results is insufficient. For example, the real action on climate change is coming from governors, mayors, corporate CEOs and community leaders. Mayors in Barcelona, Melbourne , Curitiba and Delhi are switching to cheaper and cleaner fuel sources for urban infrastructure.

As Jeffrey Sachs spelled out in his book *To Move the World: JFK's Quest for Peace* (2013), JFK's tragic death brought to a sudden end one of the greatest demonstrations in modern history of harnessing high rhetoric to grand statesmanship for genuine peace. Even at the height of the Cold War and pessimism in America in the wake of the Cuban missile crisis, Kennedy reached out both to Americans and to Nikita Khrushchev, revealing that bitter adversaries could find a way forward to reach agreement on weapons control through mutual respect. His speech was a mixture of hard and soft, tactics and strategy, emotional and intellectual, a coherent and consistent message domestically and internationally. What's more it worked. Détente was negotiated, leading eventually to the end of the Cold War.

A quick review of the scandals and conflicts around the world shows that concepts of reputation, relationships and responsibility, dialogue and diplomacy are not being taken seriously enough in isolation, let alone strategically. These concepts will be a recurring theme of this book.

The problems are numerous and complex, yet where are the leaders when we need them? These authors are hopeful that whether in business, politics, (private or public), or third sector, all needing to be led for stakeholder value, there are potential leaders everywhere who, in small ways, can make the difference. Leadership is a relational concept. Leaders need followers or more accurately collaborators to be effective. As examples in this chapter have illustrated, stakeholders, employees, consumers, citizens, communities will insist upon it. But navigating the new 'normal' will not be easy.

Summary

1.   As a result of the diffusion of power, greater interdependence and interconnectedness between government, business and civil society, capitalism's role should be broadened and its economic model adapted.

2.   Corporations should be reengineered to embrace shared economic and social value.

3.   This requires new kinds of leaders, especially for business, engaging with the broader stakeholder community, summed up by the term 'collaborative diplomacy'.

4.   This can be achieved by smarter enterprises embedding a culture of collaboration, involving listening and learning and where vision and values are aligned.

5.   A new mind-set is needed that 'joins the dots', uses 'right and left brain' and acquires new, especially 'soft' skills – people and communication. There should be a greater focus on the mind-sets and capabilities of the team to balance that of the systems and structures to implement change management.

6.   In a stakeholder-centric environment, where trust is paramount, leaders need to be authentic.

PART II
Redefining the Purpose of Business

Chapter 2

Ethical Business is Sustainable Business

The increasing strains on life and nature, society's accelerating complexity, and diversity resulting from global interdependence and interconnectedness has piled on the pressure of organisational decision making and management of organisations. Companies are the building blocks of the modern world, yet too many are operating at the fringes of morality. With question marks over senior executive compensation and growing inequalities and trust in business and business leaders at an all time low, the question must be asked, what steps are needed to rebuild credibility? Has there been too much focus on return on capital rather than corporate behaviour? Doing 'the right thing' is complicated in today's market place and relationships with stakeholders, when operating across countries, especially in high-context cultures, remains a challenge. A strong moral compass can be strong preventative medicine when managers, and especially leaders, are struggling in times of change, crisis and confusion. What are the implications for corporate governance, can we learn from the experiences of different countries and what is the broader role of business? Sometimes it seems as if business exists purely to enrich a small elite, yet with their resources and expertise business can 'help fix the world'. But how? And by collaborating with whom? Despite great strides made by some corporations in terms of adding social value and adopting greater integrated reporting in pursuit of transparency, there is dire need for more dialogic and diplomatic approaches to stakeholder engagement, involving a relational approach. There are ways to make money sustainably by linking responsible behaviour to business fundamentals, as this chapter explores.

Nothing struck at the heart of the debate around maximising shareholder value versus balancing stakeholder value more than when the CEO of Barclays Bank, Antony Jenkins, (appointed in 2013 to clean up its reputation, battered by events during the financial crisis of 2008/9) was asked in an interview on BBC radio in the UK if fraudulent bankers generally should be sent to prison, and responded to the effect: 'That's a matter for society' (BBC Radio 4, *Today* programme).

As an after thought the interviewer reflected that he thought corporations are part of society. Which is surely the point?

Community with a Purpose

The lesson from that financial crisis is that banks have wider responsibilities than to shareholders alone, especially as they underpin the global economy. Apart from anything else they have responsibilities to support economic recovery and enhance the stability of the financial system. Fortunately the bank's decision, prompted by the UK regulator, to clean up its financial act made both more likely. But this CEO, as he admits, has a long way to go before the culture of the bank can be changed. Barclays has certainly learned some lessons. Let's hope that others do too. British management guru, Charles Handy, summed it up nicely in a seminal article 'What is Business For? (2003): 'In a knowledge society, good business is a community with a purpose, not a piece of property.' Handy was making the point in the midst of the Enron and Worldcom scandals in the US that the share price is too narrow a metric for defining corporate success when trust in business is at an all-time low and confidence in those who lead it cracking. Tomorrow's Company made the point in 2014 that 'we need to see beyond treating people as things because the cultural challenge we now face is how we create value together'.

Shareholder/Stakeholder Conundrum

The relatively new Archbishop of Canterbury, Justin Welby, in one of his first acts made an assault on pay-day money lenders in the UK, not by trying to legislate them out of business (he is a member of the House of Lords second chamber), but by competing with them via a network of parish churches offering up non-profit credit unions. However, it turned out that the Church of England's pension fund was investing in high-interest rate lending companies. Of course these companies do play an economic role, but tend to feed off poverty. It happened despite these kinds of organisations being on a blacklist of 'unethical' investments. This example, although obviously an inconsistency in the Church's operations, illustrates the shareholder versus stakeholder conundrum perfectly. Pharmaceutical giant GSK has been reeling from fraud allegations in China relating to bribery, in marked contrast to its 2012 annual report, which stated, 'operating in a responsible way is essential for the commercial success of the company'. Again this shows an inconsistency between the vision and the practice. Admittedly it is sometimes difficult to maintain standards across cultures, particularly in markets like China which are fraught with ethical dilemmas. Civil society has certainly become very firm and deep rooted in parts of China with NGOs making bolder statements and sometimes bargaining with the state. No longer do NGOs need to find a government 'sponsor', with some of them taking on the state's burden. So China, with its authoritarian capitalism system, will be a good case study of the relationship between the state, business (local and foreign) and civil society, including NGOs. Chinese leaders are well aware that the state of the environment is a major cause of social unrest in the country, as well as a cause of a range of health and other issues. Chinese public opinion has recognised that these issues are systemic and activists recognise that good environmental policy depends on open and accurate information. As a result grassroots pressure is mounting for the environment to serve as a general model for the rule of law and official accountability. China serves as a prime example of the issue this chapter addresses, namely that the way we are producing and consuming is unsustainable, meaning things cannot go on as they are. Indeed the economy is relatively privileged to the environment and society, due to several hundred years of industrialisation. This needs to be rebalanced as we consume less and share more, collaborate while also competing so as to create sustainable value.

In an Ideal World ...

When British Prime Minister David Cameron entered office he promoted a concept called 'The Big Society', making a distinction between state intervention and government, business and civil society collaboration. Welby's experiment, as the UK's *The Times* columnist Danny Finkelstein wrote at the time: 'Will show whether social institutions, combining moral force and economic ingenuity can succeed. It will be the biggest test yet of The Big Society' (2013).

'Moral' force is a big word for capitalism to swallow, particularly the Anglo-Saxon variety, but perhaps an appeal can be made to 'economic ingenuity'. At least progress has been made with corporate responsibility programmes 'de rigeur' in many large corporations. Reporting initiatives abound, some of which have been mandated, especially in the environmental area. Some companies operate beyond compliance, although sometimes the spectre of quarterly earnings brings the vision crashing back to reality.

Long-Termism

Companies are the building blocks of the modern world. America has 6,000,000 of them and the number of Chinese companies increased by 80 per cent between 2004 and 2008. Yet why have so many of them gone up in flames? The doctrine of shareholder primacy is dangerous when combined with managers hired to make decisions on their behalf, with long-termism needing to be built into the DNA of companies. The then Chairman of Cadbury, a British food firm bought by US Kraft after a bloody takeover battle, noted that individuals controlling shares which they had owned for only a short while determined the destiny of a company built up over 200 years! This is Anglo-Saxon capitalism. Many German companies take a longer view as some of them are partly owned by foundations. Today business is expected to engage, not just with investors, governments and regulators, but also with a vast crowd of poorly defined newcomers – its stakeholders. However, almost anyone can become one and they define themselves. A Google search on genetically modified (GM) foods will produce millions of hits. Even endangered species can become stakeholders if the media and pressure groups appoint them on their behalf. You cannot please all the people all the time. Boards however do need to be consistent and transparent as a point of departure.

The stakeholder approach has still not yet taken off in a formal way, certainly not fully superseding the shareholder primacy model. Though it would be true to say that a narrower 'stakeholder relationship' model is now commonplace. Vincent Neate, Head of Sustainability at KPMG, has commented: 'The relationship is the last driver of sustainable business value the gurus have not really shone their light upon. We have exhausted the possibilities of improving me or you. We have to get to grips with improving us' (Tomorrow's Company Report, 2014).

The Bigger Picture

One of the reasons that more progress has not been made is a failure to see the bigger picture. In our society, including academic and bureaucratic, prestige accrues to those who study some narrow aspect of a problem. In addition to specialists we need those who can spot strong interactions and entanglements of the different dimensions, and then take a crude look at the whole.

The dots this book is trying to connect are leadership, stakeholders (including shareholders), value and values, a responsible approach, employing dialogue and diplomacy.

In the UK, despite the state being withdrawn from many services, with the Church, political parties and trade unions also in relative decline, the question must be asked, what is the broader role of business? A second question, reflected in the debate about where corporations pay taxes, is what is the governance of multinational corporations?

Steven Johnson in his book *Future Perfect: The Case for Progress in a Networked Age* (2012) outlined how some companies in the US, which paid their employees higher wages than their competitors and resisted the pull of immense senior executive packages, not only stayed in business, but outperformed the market. In the ten years leading up to 2006, these 12 or so publicly quoted stakeholder firms generated a far higher return compared to Standard and Poor 500's 122 per cent return! It cannot be good that in the US senior management are earning nearly 300 times that of the average employee? It has been argued that economic recovery in the West will only widen the rich–poor divide, with the middle classes squeezed. In America, profits as a share of gross domestic product (GDP) have risen from less than four per cent in the mid-1980s to 11 per cent in 2013. 'A statistic that would gladden the heart of nineteenth-century robber barons,' is how stakeholder proponent John Plender put it (1997). Of course there's always a tug of war between labour and capital, except now, at least in the West, employment isn't rising. The rich have benefitted from all the extra money pumped into these economies, because it has inflated the 'value' of all their assets, from stocks to houses. Meanwhile, competition from China and elsewhere, the replacement of certain jobs by robots and computers, as well as outsourcing to lower-wage cost countries means these trends will continue. What is true for the US is also true for Europe, and even countries such as Singapore where the cost of living has soared, leading to growing inequalities of income. Apart from higher domestic debt is the wall of money coming Singapore's way as the city-state establishes itself as a global centre for managing money. We are not campaigners, but a wildly unequal society is surely indefensible in moral terms (anywhere in the world), not to mention 'unsustainable? The Singapore Government has at last recognised that it must create a new narrative with its citizens, as well as address questions of its national development, in particular inequalities.

Whole Foods Market Co-CEO John Mackey (Mackey and Sisodia, 2013) made the point that business leaders should recognise that their companies are not machines but part of a complex, evolving system with multiple stakeholders. Profit is one of the most important purposes, but not the sole purpose of corporate existence. He argued that the best way to maximise long-term profit is to create value for the entire, interdependent system.

'This will happen when firms no longer run as politburos or fiefdoms', when 'peer progressive' values are applied to corporate structures, balancing a more decentralised network with 'top-down' command and control structures. It is ironic that Facebook's mission is to build a bottom-up network, while retaining a top-down structure, at least in terms of shareholding. Johnson cited employee-owned businesses, such as some in Silicon Valley, as good examples of better-performing companies, because you have two stakeholders in one.

In light of corporate scandals exemplified by the financial crash, you would think that all the above is obvious – the excesses of Fred Goodwin at Royal Bank of Scotland and the fraud of Bernie Madoff show greed is not good. 'Doing well by doing good' is the mantra of firms such as Virgin, Walmart, Starbucks and Standard Chartered Bank, (indeed it is the advertising strapline of the latter). Standard Chartered Bank states in its annual Sustainability Report: 'As an international bank, we have the capability and network to help tackle the environmental, social and economic challenges faced by society.' The trouble is that there is no universally accepted set of professional guidelines for management which reconcile the stakeholder and shareholder approach. Long-term leadership is needed to handle business in socially constructive ways.

Embedding Ethical Behaviour

Corporate citizenship – a commitment to ethical behaviour in business strategy, operations and culture – has been on the periphery of corporate governance and Board leadership, linked mainly to corporate reputation. However, in today's globalised and interconnected world, stakeholders have come to recognise that the trinity of economics, environment and ethics need to be in alignment if companies are to achieve long-term sustainability. Corporate citizenship links directly to three fundamental functions of Boards – protecting stakeholder rights and interests, managing risk and creating long-term business value. Fortunately the OECD Principles and the UN Global Compact exist to integrate rights, legitimacy and information, reflecting stakeholders' expectations into Board strategies. Yet the composition of Boards does not reflect these broader obligations.

Making Money Sustainably

Is there a better way of rebooting capitalism? Bill Gates became a philanthropist, helping to eradicate disease in Africa and India, after making millions in the traditional system while head of Microsoft. Richard Branson is investing in green energy technologies while his airline Virgin contributes to the depletion of the ozone layer, albeit providing an important service. Business writers Matthew Bishop and Michael Green are optimistic: 'For every blinkered banker chasing short-term profit, there has probably been a social entrepreneur, an ethical investor or a philanthropist trying to find a more sustainable way of making money' (Bishop and Green, 2010). Business globally needs to have a debate about this. Above all we need an economically competent citizenry and a media that deals with trends and small incremental steps, rather than covering just the big, negative events. Many issues are global, unable to be resolved by one institution, yet if these institutions worked in partnership they could be. In Africa and India there are great examples of international companies working with local authorities and NGOs, particularly on health care issues. It is also true that most institutions view the world from inside out, when their prism should be outside in, with a greater emphasis on stakeholders.

Collaboration between governments, business and civil society is more relevant than ever in these complex environments. In an increasingly networked world this should all become easier. In failed states business cannot succeed. Governments alone cannot provide all the public goods and services required and increasingly demanded by citizens. However, there is growing expectation that companies should take into account the impact of their activities on the wider communities and on the people on whom their businesses depend. Changing patterns of global trade mean companies source goods in low-cost countries, but are now deemed responsible for labour conditions and working practices, for example clothes in Bangladesh and coffee in East Africa. Good governance has an ethical dimension, as well as partnerships with government (national and local) and civil society in all its guises (increasingly virtual). Francis Yeoh, Managing Director of Malaysian infrastructure company YTL, has argued that government subsidisation of basic services on offer in Asia – water, energy, transport, Internet access – to ensure quality is not sustainable and that they should be opened up to private competition. In this, the Association of South East Asian Nations (ASEAN) needs to play a pivotal role, so that citizens from countries such as Laos and Myanmar can benefit from world-class public services. Interestingly, while few are calling for the end of capitalism, there is a growing demand for the reform of existing business models.

Business ethics is about relationships, those between business and society. It concerns purpose and values, adopting a stakeholder and issues management approach. A first step is to gain an understanding of the environmental forces that influence 'stakes' – economic, technological, political, social, legal and demographic (note the debate on immigration within the EU and the impact of migration in many parts of the world of those escaping strife or poverty). As part of mapping stakeholders' stakes and interrelationships, it is important to define each stakeholder's ethics in relation to the issue. 'Collaborative strategies' will develop from these. This in turn enables dialogue from a higher-ground perspective so as to reach a mutually desirable goal.

Business ethics provides principles and guidelines, assisting people to make informed choices that balance economic interests with social responsibilities. Being able to reflect on stakeholders' interest can better inform the moral dimension of personal decisions. Laws, of course, are often insufficient to cover 'grey' areas and free-market mechanisms are not equipped with a moral compass. We do seem to spend much of the time 'dancing in the grey zone'.

Enron's ethics code was based on respect, integrity, communication and excellence. What went wrong was a failure of the top leaders, arrogance, hubris pervading its culture, not to mention complicity of the firm's financial advisers. (Four days before Enron announced big losses, a senior partner of Andersons ordered the shredding of all relevant papers.) Nevertheless, a few bad apples should not make us pessimistic about the possibilities. Stakeholder theory argues that corporations should treat all their constituencies fairly and that doing so enables them to perform better in the market place. This should embrace not just urgency and power, but also legitimacy. A subset of ethical principles – trust and trustworthiness – can result in significant competitive advantage. According to American academic Francis Fukuyama in his book *Trust: The Social Virtues and the Creation of Prosperity* (2005), trustworthiness consists of ability, benevolence and integrity, the building up of what he calls 'social capital'. This allows agreements to be reached without reducing everything to bargaining or formal contracting. Trust is a concept running like a stream through this book.

According to a McKinsey Global Survey (July 2014), company leaders are rallying behind sustainability, believing it to be increasingly important to business strategy. The challenge will be integrating it as a core business process. Many respondents noted that companies are not pursuing the reputation-building aspects that would maximise financial value, despite reputation having the most value potential. Reputation is directly linked to trust. One of the issues here is that there is a lack of clarity around reputation management. However, a positive sign is that 'sustainability' leaders set themselves apart via target setting, a clear strategy supported by a broad coalition of senior managers.

Dialogue and Diplomacy

Relational approaches are preferable to power approaches, involving dialogue in negotiation and mediation. Ethical reasoning should be an important element of managing stakeholders and broader issues, thus narrowing the gap between company action and stakeholder expectations.

A key lesson for the stakeholder corporation is listening, which is implicit in dialogue. 'Cycles of inclusion' – diagnosis, dialogue and audit – involve what is known as 'double-loop learning'. This is a process of sensing, scanning and monitoring the external environment, comparing this to operating norms, reflecting on the appropriateness and only then deciding what is the appropriate action. Which in turn requires on-going debate and innovation. It is the opposite of a bureaucratic approach. Networked organisations tend to be better at this process. Top-down models are less than optimal, compared to double-loop learning, knowledge creating and collaborative strategies. Whereas in a discussion different views are presented and defended, in dialogue different views are presented so as to discover a new view. True dialogue involves listening, respect and willingness to change.

Although inclusive relationships may be accomplished in several ways, normative interpretation of stakeholder theory is the most appropriate methodology to enable moral judgements to be made as an integral part of the decision-making process. Principles need to be weaved into the fabric of excellence. Profits should be a reflection, not of corporate greed, but a vote of confidence from society that what is offered by the firm is *valued*.

Combining Economic with Social Value

Given that privately held corporations are larger than many countries and, simply by entering a market, add value to that country – 'a rising tide lifts all boats' – and there are guidelines for managing morality via internationally agreed codes of conduct, many corporations still operate in the margins of morality. Here we are not talking simply about the extreme examples such as Enron. This is a result of history, culture and governmental norms not being uniform. Sometimes a local country style is adopted (when in Rome), sometimes an Empire style reminiscent of the Colonial era; only rarely a cosmopolitan or globally consistent style. At least more recent reporting and transparency initiatives help. However, as business and ethics are largely separate and business dogma continues to assert the primacy of shareholder value, how can companies be expected both to fuel free-market economies and help provide health care, education and protect privacy?

This is why, as ethics theorist Robert Phillips noted in his article 'The Environment as Stakeholder' (2000), the stakeholder principle is based on 'fairness'. He referred to five ethical decision-making principles. First 'utilitarianism' calculates all costs and benefits, taking into account duty to all; 'productivism' views CSR in terms of rational self-interest; 'philanthropy' adopts a free-market view but nevertheless believes in a moral responsibility towards less-advantaged members of society via charity; and finally, 'progressivism' and 'ethical idealism' are the two so-called social responsibility modes in the stakeholder model. This group believes that socially responsible corporations have a competitive advantage in their ability to attract quality employees and their broader reputation will result in higher sales. Reputation is not an abstract concept, but a tangible corporate asset, linked to relationships and responsible behaviour.

Corporate Responsibility Link to Business Fundamentals

CSR is evolving. Gone are the days when it was mainly about managing corporate reputation. It is now more about business strategy.

The problem with the natural environment, arguably the biggest stakeholder, the subject of much debate in this area, is that stakeholder theory deals only with human beings. This despite the fact that 'sustainability' implies being a trustee of future generations of human beings. Naturally, local communities operate in the physical environment, so companies and local communities should work together to protect it. The debate is really over the global community, which some argue is rather like 'telescopic philanthropy', that is, that companies should first pay heed to their local backyards. Although the Indian national Government's new law (August 2013), expecting corporations to give 2 per cent of their net profits to CSR projects, is probably not the way to do it. But it's a start. Transparency and accountability is likely to be the better way.

A time existed when corporations exploited the environment as a free and unlimited resource. But this time is gone as a result of the depletion of the earth's resources – air, water, land, climate change, smog in Beijing, pollution of seas, toxic waste – as Al Gore has reminded us. The utilitarian ethic – calculating costs and benefits – is insufficient to justify continuing negligence and abuse. We need to ask, what is a fair market price for destruction of the Brazilian rain forests, melting of ice caps in the North Pole, making life impossible for polar bears, and extreme weather affecting farmers and whole communities? The list goes on.

Inclusive Stakeholder Relations

An innovative move by some corporations is to include environmental safety practices in the strategic enterprise and supply chain dimensions of their industrial activities and practices. Leadership requires involvement in stakeholder relations because business involves making choices and ethical decisions on issues such as harmful products, oil spills, lawsuits and layoffs. Moral courage and credibility are essential leader attributes. James Collins' five-year research project (published in 2011) on 11 'good to great' companies revealed a rare, but particular leadership approach, devoid of ego and self-interest; a blend of personal humility yet professional will. Coupled with this kind of leadership, a firm which wishes to raise the level of human conduct, needs a values-based organisational culture. Novartis talks about achieving a strong sustainable performance based on 'continuous innovation'. Fujitsu does its bit for tropical rainforest regeneration in Sabah, Malaysia while at the same time surveying the wildlife to assess the changes in biodiversity. Nike is making more clothes from polyester produced by recycling bottles. It has also shared its Materials Sustainability Index with the trade body, which represents 30 per cent of the global market for clothes and footwear. Yet there are still many Indonesian companies, in cahoots with local government and entrepreneurs, causing permanent degradation of natural forests, with the inevitable annual air pollution of neighbouring countries and its accompanying health and diplomatic issues. Survival International has provided evidence that foreign companies have done deals with the Ethiopian Government to build a dam which, apart from being illegal, will have a negative impact on the ecosystem and also displace indigenous tribes.

The World Business Council on Sustainable Development asserts that CSR relies on government, business and civil society sharing a common long-term vision to address economic, social and environmental issues. AVIVA, the UK insurance company, switched its CSR emphasis from 'champion' to 'catalyst' of street children, engaging the whole business alongside community experts for maximum impact. Singapore telecommunications firm STARHUB tries to strengthen social cohesion in disadvantaged families on the grounds that its product may have played an indirect role in eroding ties among family members. This author (RH) has observed, while consulting and teaching in

Asia, that some companies are becoming committed to causes with sustained long-term initiatives.

Shining a Light

Transparency linked to technological innovation and global competitiveness can be transformative because it means that stakeholders have information which can be shared through the network. So maybe some of these corrupt practices in fragile countries can eventually be wiped out. Richness of information has also led to codification of standards relating to social and environmental practice. One of the key benefits is that it shines a light on corporate and governmental malpractice. The need for sustainable development has piled on the pressure for corporations to involve multi-stakeholder groups in certain decisions. The Marine Stewardship Council (MSC), a partnership that sets standards for the fishing industry, is a classic example of this approach. As values shift, so too can companies adjust their strategies, attracting stakeholders who share similar beliefs, including shareholders, some of whom only invest in ethical stocks.

The late Anita Roddick, founder of one the early sustainable companies, Body Shop, wrote in the Foreword to *The Stakeholder Corporation* (Wheeler and Sillanpaa, 1997): 'Large companies around the world are beginning to recognise that to be legitimate requires companies to be proactive not passive. It takes a little courage to shed the command and control mentality, to see your stakeholders as sources of strength rather than instability'. Loyal relationships are increasingly dependent on how a company is perceived to create 'added value' beyond commercial transactions. This is a crucial link between reputation and responsibility. Inclusive stakeholder relations will eventually become one of the most important determinants of commercial viability and business success. It is interesting that Germany and Japan have tended to adopt a broader view of stakeholder interest – a consensus rather than a confrontational model. Again this is partly based on history, partly culture and partly legal. For example, an employee who devotes his life to a business has a morally larger stake than a shareholder who only has one short-term interest. The Japanese are adherents to the concept of 'Kyosei' developed by a former chairman of Canon cameras, which translates as 'Working Together for the Common Good'. The stakeholder model, espoused by the Japanese system (if not by all companies within it) fits in with the broadly accepted ethical considerations.

The power and purpose of corporations is being challenged as global economic growth, disparities in wealth, tensions between the US and China, and concomitant social challenges, have begged the questions – what should the expectations of companies and their leaders be and what are the skills needed? Governments and public sector organisations face similar challenges.

In the book *Unfolding Stakeholder Thinking* (Andriof et al., 2003), a group of European academics identified that the debate about sustainable development has shifted to accountability and verifiable reporting. They refer to several high-profile companies such as Shell, Levi-Strauss, Nike and Body Shop that have joined the ranks of 'progressive' companies. Why? Because they have listened and responded to their various internal and external stakeholders, including critics. At the same time, NGOs such as WWF, Oxfam, Amnesty International and Greenpeace have embraced a more collaborative approach to their relations with business – which does not rule out retaining a 'campaigning' element as well. This climate has allowed for, or may even have resulted from, enhanced inclusiveness, partnership and dialogue. Whatever the case, mind-sets have begun to change. But there is a long road ahead.

When Shell revised its general business principles to reflect its growing commitment to the natural environment and human rights, its message was Profit, People and Planet. However, this did not satisfy environmental and human rights activists. Nike also, despite a brand image campaign, failed to counteract claims of sweatshop labour, tainting it and its products. The dialogic model, which implies partnership and collaboration, is little examined in the stakeholder literature, because genuine dialogue is geared towards mutual education, joint problem-solving and true relationship building. This was summarised by Millicent Danker, to whom this book is dedicated, as 'co-created meaning'.

A Holistic Approach

So while this requires further examination, it is true that if in the 1980s and 1990s corporate responsibility focused on community involvement, there is now a more holistic approach to sustainable development. But governance and the field of multi-stakeholder dialogue require a particular kind of leadership that is rare. The ability to conceptualise and make sense of change is a key skill of 'servant leaders', who do not trivialise complex problems and impose over-simplistic solutions on them. Steve Downing (2008/9), a specialist in sustainability at Henley Business School makes the point that 'they lead assuming an intelligent audience and because they do not impose their own quick fixes, they invite those around them to take responsibility for solutions'. From being relatively simple questions of legal and financial relations, interrelationships between an organisation and the social and geopolitical environment are now more complex, dynamic and ambiguous, requiring more reflective sensitivity. There are more holistic paradigms now, which is a challenge for leaders to wrap their minds around, given the usual siloed approach.

Sustainability is not mutually exclusive to creating returns for shareholders, even though it is our contention that shareholders do not own the company in any meaningful sense. The reason is because they have other holdings and are impermanent. Leading-edge companies integrate strategy, process and people across social, economic and environmental domains, other things being equal providing excellent returns and a lower risk profile. Responsible corporations must recognise an evolving social contract that stems from the need for partnerships, combined with a significant leadership role, collaborating with government and civil society, for the common good. One of the problems is that companies list their top factors as employee talent, long-term vision, corporate culture, stakeholder engagement and capacity to innovate, yet they actually manage based on factors such as growth, sales and share price. This has become a vicious cycle as business schools still provide students with the tools to maximise returns rather than balance stakeholder expectations, even though some are beginning to adopt a more stakeholder approach

Corporate responsibility has long recognised that corporations have responsibilities beyond their narrow duties. There is now a call for leadership in the global public sphere, from peer group networks from the US to China, India to the EU. In this new century it is business that has broader power as that of the nation state shrinks. So surely what is needed are creative social initiatives involving the private sector?

Social Enterprises

'Maybe one day all corporations will become "social enterprises"', an executive of the UK Institute of Directors (IOD) told this author (RH). This is particularly the case in less-developed countries where economic development and environmental/social issues are intimately linked. With the evolving sustainable development paradigm, which involves horizontal and lateral networks of collaboration, intricate relationships between private and public organisations, civil society and government are required. Public and quasi-public organisations can play a role creating businesses, as in the case of waste management in Brazil.

Incidentally, the city of Curitiba in this country (population two million) has one of the highest rates of recycling in the world.

C.K. Prahalad and Allen Hammond (2002) argue that corporations could create a more sustainable world by tapping the four billion people earning less than two dollars per day, a vast potential market. After all, poor farmers in El Salvador use telecentres to negotiate the sale of their crops via the Internet. Women in rural India use GSM cell phones to conduct small-scale business. Kenyan teenagers are being trained as web designers.

One of the most important challenges facing civilisation is the explosive growth of cities. Two hundred years ago 2 per cent lived in them, whereas in the next two decades 70 per cent are likely to. There are collaboration requirements in education, health, infrastructure and energy. A scheme to recycle human effluent in Nairobi has improved sanitation and made money. This has involved local entrepreneurs, NGOs, local authorities and Western business. (We review stakeholder communities in cities in a later chapter.)

Progress and Pitfalls

Several case histories illustrate some of the excellent collaboration being undertaken as well as some of the pitfalls:

1. IBM has instigated a programme to reinvent education in America's inner cities – working with the public schools has proved that community needs are no longer the dumping ground for obsolete equipment but opportunities to test ideas and demonstrate new technologies as well as to find and serve new markets. To sustain results, however, it needed a mutual commitment, moving beyond corporate responsibility to what has been termed social innovation. This is when companies view involvement from a research and development perspective. (Incidentally the company is also impressive in Japan and its reputation has soared, having created a separate product development team to build devices that allow disabled people to live more independently.)

2. Tata Steel on its website says it is 'doing the right thing in every aspect of its business'. It has five core values – integrity, understanding, excellence, unity and responsibility. According to the company – 'tackling challenges of sustainability follows

naturally from this ethical stance'. The company's definition of sustainability incidentally is 'an enduring and balanced approach to economic activity, environmental responsibility and social benefit'. The company asserts that steel is sustainable because it is 'truly recyclable'. Its approach to CO_2 emissions, efficiency, waste management and energy-saving products ensures that the company can tackle relevant sustainability challenges while satisfying all relevant stakeholders. It believes that a spin-off is 'good PR' in a globally competitive market place, adding value to performance as well acting valuably in its environmental impacts.

3.   Anglo-American Corporation launched an internal stakeholder dialogue process at its Quellaveco copper project in South Peru. It was set up to address civil society concerns about water impacts in an arid region. Eighteen months of detailed dialogue concluded with commitments on infrastructure, local hiring and wildlife protection, including joint monitoring of compliance. The company believes that the key to this process was listening and the result has been deeper understanding. More broadly, its Annual Sustainability Report accepts that business has never been under such scrutiny, not least in the mining sector, as a result of greater transparency and accountability. The company has worked with trade unions and government on health and safety issues in South Africa. It has cooperated with municipalities to provide basic services in local communities, cooperating with NGOs and development institutions in the areas of energy, housing and water. It believes the key to sustainability is not handouts but inclusion, investing in employment and education.

4.   Shell learned its lessons from the battering to its reputation during the controversy over the disposal of the Brent Spar oil rig in the UK's North Sea, condemned by Greenpeace, as well as its neutral stance to military assassinations in Nigeria quite a few years ago, despite the scale of its operations there. It achieved this, following a full-scale review, by moving beyond its economic rationality and scientific expertise culture to a more outside-in, proactive one. This was thanks to what it describes as 'transformative learning'. Over the years Shell has been an advocate of 'scenario planning'. In 2011, in the wake of the financial crisis, the company released a report titled 'Signals and Signposts', which analysed long-term energy scenarios in an era of volatility. Most recently, the pressures

as a result of the interdependence between water, food and energy became a discussion with stakeholders titled 'The Stress Nexus Conversation'. Shell realised it needed to look at these issues in a joined up way, involving stakeholders in a dialogue.

5.   Coca-Cola has won awards for its public–private partnerships related to water sustainability initiatives in developing countries. Since 2004, the company has been accused by activists and several government organisations of creating environmental problems by depleting groundwater tables when making its beverages (both directly and in the supply chain). It therefore proposed to become water neutral by 2010, focusing on three core areas – reduction, recycling and replenishment. It has made some progress in this regard in 20 countries, but some activists still complain it is nothing more than 'greenwashing'. Some critics opine that its efforts towards launching several rainwater harvesting projects in India were part of its 'public relations strategy', certainly insufficient to offset the water used up by its operations.

6.   China Mobile is included in the Dow Jones Sustainability Index, one of the few Chinese mainland companies included at the moment. For this company sustainability means having a framework in place that pursues working with stakeholders to promote corporate and societal sustainability, for example via resource efficiency and promoting social equality involving technology and service. Their emphasis is on an 'information-enhanced future', particularly between rural and urban areas.

This is all progress, if with some pitfalls. We have seen companies arrive with an aspiration slogan, for example 'BP – Beyond Petroleum', along with a CEO speech extolling the company's commitment to a better and responsible future. As if on cue an oil spill happened in the Gulf of Mexico, the responsibility of that same company. This incident and its unsubtle handling by the company's then CEO became a 'cause célèbre'. While not every incident or crisis can be avoided, this tells these authors that there is sometimes an enormous gap between vision and values. Corporate culture has a lot to do with it, possibly in this instance an emphasis of cost over safety.

A CEO's leadership is crucial in overseeing a feisty dialogue between environmental/ social involvements and business functions. This should align corporate values with appropriate causes, a key word being 'appropriate'.

Individual companies, even individual governments, cannot solve all the world's problems. Indeed Michael Porter and Mark Kramer (2011) believe that what they call 'philanthropy' (a somewhat narrow definition of what we are discussing) can often be the most cost-effective way for a company to improve its 'corporate context'. This means enabling it to leverage the efforts, knowledge and infrastructure of non-profits and other institutions. This reflects our view that the two go hand in hand and are mutually reinforcing.

Many companies and other institutions are shifting from social responsibility to increasing shared value – what Bill Clinton calls 'hand-ups, not hand-outs'. Certainly corporate emphasis on sustainable development beyond simply philanthropy or even corporate responsibility has evolved the thinking. Sadly, stakeholder theory has not trickled down below the few truly multinational corporations known for their advanced thinking. Unilever is perhaps the best example. Of course it is accepted there are many companies that do their bit at local level without fanfare. This problem should be grounded in the 'creation of business value'. Stakeholder theory has never really been purely about social issues. It's also about customers, employees and investors, just as sustainability is not just about environment.

The father of 'fracking' in the United States, the late George Mitchell, who from his Texas base, helped turn that country into a net exporter of natural gas (much to the chagrin of Russia and Saudi Arabia), believed in trying to find the right balance between economic growth, environmental protection and social justice. This is not a bad definition of sustainability, describing the delicate balancing of competing stakeholder interests and expectations. Indeed the broader social and environmental costs of doing business, hitherto externalized, should now to be internalised.

Earning a Licence to Grow

We need our leaders and institutions to reconceive how they build for growth. We are moving from 'earning a licence to operate' to 'earning a licence to grow', as consulting firm APCO Worldwide (2008) explain it. It is significant that a combination of scarcity and our more interconnected world have placed a premium on how we behave. It's that link between transparency and trust again.

A paragraph in the *Financial Times* (2009) caught our eye:

The idea that what business is for and its place in society has been lost in the detail. Confucius, the moral philosopher of collectivism and Adam Smith, the advocate of selfishness functioning in a moral universe, should get together to move capitalism and therefore management thinking to the next level.

The debate has begun, but the journey will be long and hard. There's no time to lose.

Summary

1.   Corporations have a big role to play in reshaping the future, which requires a broader and longer-term approach. Business, government and civil society leaders need to have a vigorous debate and collaborate more on addressing social need, developing social enterprise models.

2.   Corporate responsibility has become more strategic and stakeholder approaches adopted. But there is a gap between ideals and reality. More of an outside-in approach should be adopted, taking on board political and cultural as well as market contexts. There should be more emphasis on deep listening and learning.

3.   This requires a more holistic approach to sustainability, embracing shared economic and social value, linking inclusive relationships to adding value beyond the purely commercial.

4.   Board compositions should more accurately reflect the growing complexity of the environment, balancing the emphasis on law, regulation and finance with stakeholder negotiation skills and authentic communication. To the economic dimension should be added an ethical dimension to establish a 'licence to grow'.

5.   The fundamental task of management is to continually prove the organisation worthy of trust, relying less on information and control, and more on dialogue and diplomacy.

Chapter 3

Stakeholder Primacy: An Evolving Ecosystem of Relationships

The stakeholder approach has still not yet taken off in a formal way, and has certainly not yet superseded the shareholder primacy model. Yet the two should not be in opposition. The primary role of business has not changed across history and geographies, yet expectations have. The stakeholder concept advocates a democratic approach to business, valuing relationships with a whole new ecosystem of stakeholders, embracing state, market and civil society in a more inclusive way. Companies can be active participants in shaping the world, but need to understand the key drivers (emotional and rational), mind-sets and values that drive stakeholders. While there is much material on economic and market analysis, very little exists on cultural, psychological and relational forces important for leaders to absorb. The long-term viability of the firm depends on a delicate balance of influences and inputs, which few companies are structured or sensitised to build into their missions, strategies and operations. It doesn't only apply to private sector firms but also to government departments, state enterprises, universities, charities and NGOs. Stakeholder primacy is the way for global business and other institutions to engage and connect with people at deeper levels so that, once again, capitalism can become the world's most expansive and creative force, creating many different kinds of wealth. Perhaps by integrating stakeholder relationships and responsible activities into their strategies, business leaders can truly put the 'human' into capitalism.

In his book *The State We're In* (1995), British commentator Will Hutton argued for 'a democratic political economy' that related to the whole of British society. He criticised business for being short-termist and relentless in maximising some of the highest financial returns the world had seen. Today he's still arguing the same. Especially following the financial crisis of 2008, capitalism cannot be left to itself. Why? Because it neglects both the future and cohesion of the society in which it trades. If it's obvious in banking, it has also become so in energy, with UK customer bills nearly trebling since 2004, soaring past the international average of energy prices. Hutton's point is that the energy market is dysfunctional, hence the need to shape dynamic capitalism for the good of society, building public interest objectives and social obligations into the system. As Hutton put it: 'Efficient capitalism requires careful design and organisation, along with firms that combine a business and social purpose' (1995). Competition is a bulwark against capitalist excess, but it needs to operate within a moral context.

Reframing the Narrative

Business should remain a driver of innovation, efficiency and wealth creation, yet there is a need to reframe the narrative around timescales and socio/cultural contexts that affect and are affected by private sector business. Corporations have always had a 'licence to operate', granted by citizens via their governments. Business leaders though require a *new* mandate for the changing world. The role of business has not changed across history and geographies, namely to provide goods and services people need or want, yet expectations have, resulting from the global trends discussed in the opening chapter. In many Asian and Middle-Eastern business situations, family and government interests have dominated ownership structures, unlike the Anglo-Saxon model. State capitalism is another factor in some parts of the world, exerting pressure on companies. In the future, whatever the structure, business objectives must extend beyond simply entering new markets and expanding their customer base, to create value for a wide cross-section of stakeholders, underpinned by shared values, beyond simply the shareholder base. This demands holistic stakeholder engagement.

Post-Second World War corporatism, with its endless conflicts between business, union bosses and government forced a conversation, in Europe at least, through which capitalism was reminded about society (trade unions mainly now partly replaced by NGOs). Yet, despite giving millions to environment groups in the US, BP could not be saved from its own PR disaster in the Gulf of Mexico, waves from which are still being felt within the company (not least the heavy fine) and local communities. But at least corporatism was a collective check on our capacity to think about the long-term effects of private sector decision making.

Narrow Conceptions of Business Role

Even though the ecosystems of businesses have been transformed in today's interdependent and interconnected landscape, some leaders remain entrenched in narrow conceptions of their role. Companies are having to deal with the decline of trust, greater regulation and increasing resource scarcity. This results partly from population growth leading to migrations from richer to poorer countries and from rural to urban areas. Some businesses have accepted their broader stakeholder responsibility via CSR campaigns. Yet they are rarely integrated into corporate planning or are perceived to be simply 'public relations exercises' – PR viewed (often wrongly) as superficial. This is because the activities perceived as superficial are not embedded deeply into the business. Fortunately, efforts are underway there to standardise the metrics on non-financial reporting, which could improve the way investors rate companies' socially responsible investing. More transparency is a good start.

History teaches the dire consequences of ignoring societal concerns, from sweat shop exposés to oil spills.

Transactions or Relationships?

Sir Richard Lambert of the Banking Standards Board in the UK (*Financial Times*, 2013) has also weighed into the argument, asserting that market fundamentalism means companies maximise short-term profits while exploiting customers and that preoccupation with financial performance holds back much needed investment. (He cites the announcement in October 2013 of a new nuclear power plant being built in the UK by the French with Chinese money, with the country having little to show for it by way of advanced nuclear technology.) The obsession with revenues and profits favours transactions over relationships, thus loosening links with customers and communities. Following the recent bribery scandal in China, pharmaceutical company GSK has taken a big financial and reputational hit, recognising that the company needs to restore trust in that important market. Restoring trust implies a relational approach, which inevitably means adopting a longer-term perspective as well as a global ethical culture.

Surely business must reconnect with a sense of purpose beyond profits and growth, as the return to growth after the financial crisis alone will not solve the crisis of inequality between the global elite of billionaires and unemployed millions being experienced in North America and Europe. History did not, after all, end in 1989 with the break up of the Soviet Union's economic system as foreseen by Fukuyama (1990). Indeed economics needs to relocate itself in the humanities rather than everything being reducible to numbers. It is no longer a question of left or right, or more or less government intervention. The China Business School (CEIBS) in Shanghai believes the shareholder model to be lopsided and that state-owned enterprises can be highly successful, just as different versions of public–private partnerships or mixing philanthropy with entrepreneurialism can too. Pierre Omidyar, the founder of eBay, (the worldwide online market place) and Blake Mycoskie, the founder of TOMS shoes, fostering innovative start-ups that aim to improve the world are examples.

Creative Coalitions

Perhaps the use of 'Creative Coalitions' proposed by the Oxford Martin Commission, in which governments, business and NGOs try to deal with issues outside bureaucracies, might help. It has been proposed 'a creative coalition', for instance, on climate change, involving countries, companies, charities and cities in search of a common agenda.

In contrast to the view of companies being dominated simply by the notion of improving returns to shareholders, the stakeholder concept advocates a 'democratic' approach to business. This values relationships with a whole new ecosystem of stakeholders – interrelating state, society and the economy/ market in a more 'inclusive' way. These days, MBA students are demanding business school curricula pay more attention to long-term social and ethical sustainability. In Scandinavian social democracies this ethos is already prevalent. It is reflected in Business School courses. So it matters not whether students end up in business, a government department or a not-for-profit as there will be a focus on ethical decision making. This is much needed after the freewheeling, deregulated economic model crashed in 2008!

Ecosystem Sensitivity

In an age of disruption, with many global crises, from finance to energy and food to water, there is surely an opportunity for a better balance between self-interest of the company and that of stakeholders. Again, these two should not be in opposition but rather work together in harmony. For instance, if Africa is the future of globalisation for international investors and Africans, and if the continent is to fully reap the demographic dividend, then job creation is the key. This is predicated on education, especially for young women. As Trustee of a slum school in India and having worked with many public and private sector, international and domestic organisations in that complex and diverse country, this author (RH) knows how significant this is for productivity growth in farming and to kickstart local-level entrepreneurship. No meeting concluded without the question: 'Which NGO should we team up with and in which state is our input most valuable?' This in turn means access to finance and education, hence collaboration between the public and private sectors, predicated on a common vision. But, while there is lots of material from economic and market analysis, even from business management, there is very little on the cultural, psychological and relational forces affecting business, public policy and society. This has implications for business leadership, education and training as well as corporate cultures.

We have talked thus far about the need for a more democratic political economy and the expansion of civic engagement. This assumes the involvement of many in society. With the pace of globalisation, fuelled by electronic communications, this concept assumes new significance. Scholars talk of 'democratic deliberation'. Although a new field, deliberative dialogue is beginning to be used by different stakeholder groups within local communities and beyond. They define dialogue as 'an orientation towards constructive communication – the intention to listen'. A related process, deliberation uses 'critical thinking and reasoned argument'. Both can be used together to create what is termed 'mutual understanding', which aligns personal interests with public concerns. In order to create opportunities for 'inclusive engagement' it is also important to create a wider context for the 'conversation'. This should involve those who define themselves, whether they be in the inner circle or not. Otherwise the engagement may not be totally meaningful, the key being to build trust and form relationships.

Leader as Convenor

Hence the leadership quality deployed here is for the 'convener' to help others find their voice. Apart from listening and participants using their own language, the ability to reframe an issue is essential if stakeholders are to have a real influence over a public policy or corporate agenda. The Prince of Wales is sometimes referred to as someone with 'convening power', especially with regard to his involvement in the regeneration of a town in the UK, such as Burnley. Here, greater buy-in needs to be obtained from various stakeholders in order to 'make a difference' in that town's regeneration.

Ultimately, the scholars assert, the objective should be to create common ground for sustainable community action. In this situation, leadership plainly implies creating a narrative around common interests while also adapting to a 'diversity of stakeholder decision-making styles'. Of course common ground is not consensus, so there are risks attached to 'deliberative dialogue'. But that is the point about moving forward together; stakeholders feeling they are part of the solution. Dr Millicent Danker (in her 2012 Malaysia lectures) suggested replacing hidden agendas, manipulation and one-way communication with deeper forms of dialogue such as empathy, inclusion and listening as the foundation for collective action. The Institute for Multi-track Diplomacy describes stakeholder engagement as 'the intention not to advocate, but to inquire, not to argue, but to explore, not to convince, but to discover' (quoted in Burchell and Cook, 2006).

Nexus of Relationships

Stakeholder theory developed from the strategic management literature and was popularised with Ed Freeman's book *Strategic Management: A Stakeholder Approach* (1984), viewing the firm as a nexus of relations. These are based around the notion that business has obligations not only to shareholders, but also a wide group of stakeholders. In 2004 he emphasised the need to invest in relationships with those who have a stake in the organisation, based on shared values. While it could be argued that the terminology is relatively new outside its Anglo-Saxon heritage, the general principles have been practised in many countries for some time. (Indeed Millicent Danker's doctoral research [Henley Business School, 2011] was based on a comparison of corporate governance in the UK and Malaysia.) The German model of industrial relations and supervisory Boards is a model of stakeholder democracy, with one-third of Board members being representative of employees. Scandinavia is another example of a broader approach, reflecting principles of social democracy. Most explicitly, in Japan, and to a lesser extent South Korea, there are networks of supporting suppliers, creditors and customers known as *Keiretsu* in Japan (*Chaebol* in South Korea). These are considered the most important stakeholders. In this part of Asia this has also included employees, although the concept of 'life-time employment' has eroded in recent years. Ironically, as was shown with the Olympus case, when a new British CEO blew the whistle on corruption, sometimes this tight network can serve to conceal rather than reveal scandals until a whistle-blower shines a light on wrongdoing. As Sir Walter Scott wrote in 1808: 'Oh what a tangled web we weave when first we practice to deceive?'

Public relations firms talk to clients about the need to 'map their stakeholders', yet Freeman's definition embraces just about anyone. So, inevitably, prioritisation is required. The usual way of cutting the cake is based around power, legitimacy and urgency. For instance, if a tribesman kidnaps your executive in a remote location, then he becomes an 'urgent' stakeholder. Governments usually have more 'power' than local communities, although with use of social media the power balance is changing, as we discussed in the first chapter. 'Legitimacy' depends on your definition and relates back to questions of governance. Henley Business School has done much work on the drivers, nature and outcomes of stakeholder relations (Macmillan et al., 2004) and the link with the concept of responsibility, leading inexorably to trust. Sometimes the media are not treated as stakeholders at all, more as conduits. This is now debatable. Employees, like customers and shareholders, are usually treated as 'primary' stakeholders with local communities inserted into the 'secondary' category. But why, if both have a role in minimising environmental pollution around a plant?

The Reputation Institute (2013) argues that to be fully prepared to navigate in today's 'reputation economy' companies must harness a thorough understanding of their stakeholder ecosystems in order to drive behaviours that will lead to sustainable growth. Indeed, there is no doubt a symbiotic relationship between corporate governance, corporate responsibility, corporate reputation and stakeholder relationships exists. Certainly, more proactive and structured stakeholder dialogue initiatives have become an increasingly important management issue in recent years. But it should be integrated into management thinking and decision making, leading to better governance, performance and reporting. To be trustworthy requires credibility, hence the need for authentic leadership and communications around it.

The Stakeholder Engagement Process: Case History

A Working Paper on Stakeholder Engagement (INSEAD, 2013), focusing on research with Gap Inc., illustrated the link between leadership, sustainability, ethics and responsible behaviour. The context was charges of labour rights abuses and environmental harm. This is increasingly common for major brands sourcing in today's globally expanded supply chains, often representing reputational risks at the least. It described how the company transformed from a typical compliance-based approach to a more proactive stakeholder engagement strategy. This involved: 1) mapping to win internal commitment; 2) identifying the material issues; 3) defining objectives; 4) resolving issues collaboratively; and 5) embedding engagement.

However, as the paper explained, the particular approach required a different mind-set, transitioning from risk aversion to partnership, from quick fixes to sustainable solutions. The process helped the company anticipate the future, facilitate trust as well as improve its reputation. The authors suggested: 'It provides a deeper understanding of a company's obligations to its stakeholders consistent with its commitment to corporate social responsibility.' Companies such as Gap Inc., while not immune to violations in their supply chain, are nevertheless better prepared to deal with them via an 'action not words' approach. In this case study of research in several developing countries, stakeholder engagement was viewed as a sophisticated way to address complex supply chain and other sustainability problems, and as a result to be better prepared for the inevitable crisis.

The Gap frame of mind following this exercise, after years of protest against it (even prior to the 1999 WTO anti-globalisation protest in Seattle), is to treat stakeholders, not as 'noise makers', but as 'critical friends'. Media reports spoke of sales improvements as the company increasingly leveraged social and environmental awareness programmes to appeal to its younger clientele. Companies such as Gap Inc. have found this to be an opportunity rather than a risk. Indeed this resulted in the Ethical Trading Initiative (an alliance of companies, trade unions and voluntary organisations), involving many of its competitors too. More recently this kind of communication has evolved to be more dialogic and solutions oriented. Needless to say it involved 'deep listening' and 'relationship building' skills.

Incidentally Gap Inc. discovered that one particularly effective tool is the multi-stakeholder dialogue approach, involving NGOs, academics, government and trade unions (a tool referred to earlier in the book). This had the additional impact of providing the company with 'eyes' globally as well as a dense network of intelligence, including an informal complaint mechanism on issues such as underage employees or the impact of HIV/AIDS. Boundary spanners were used – those who understood the corporate as well as the civil society discourse. Indeed the INSEAD research revealed that listening, empathy and transparency are critical skills. This was reinforced by Burchell and Cook (2006): 'These systems of stakeholder dialogue are part of corporate learning as companies seek to strengthen their social capital via socially responsible practices.' Shell learned the lesson, following its Brent Spar rig decommissioning experience, that led to uproar among customers, NGOs and media pundits, notably in Germany and the UK, that listening to stakeholders totally transformed their approach to the wider ecosystem of stakeholders.

Managing Complex Externalities

Thus new leadership is required in the boardroom – soft skills alongside hard, which are vital for stakeholder engagement, let alone building and maintaining trusted relationships. Historically it was important to have a particular skill in marketing or finance, understand a particular sector of the business and preferably experience of a key foreign market. These days, while these remain important, a part of the architecture of leadership should include the ability to manage more complex externalities. These include deepening and widening engagement, often with those outside the comfort zone. It is essential that engagement be embedded within the organisation, which is partly a function of process and culture, but particularly of leadership. The paradox is that the greater the transparency, the greater the danger of being accused and targeted, compared to those with a lower profile. Transparency should be seen as an opportunity for thought-leadership.

Recognising the business case for sustainability, the European Commission has asked companies to increase transparency by reporting in a more integrated manner. This is due to the interdependence of social, environmental and business strategy issues. Integrated reporting is fast replacing pure sustainability reporting, which is at least a move in the right direction.

A Strategic Approach

A report on the future of stakeholder engagement, based on research among 130 European organisations (Brunswick Insight, 2013), found that while stakeholder engagement is considered to be extremely important, at most organisations surveyed stakeholder engagement tends to be ad-hoc not strategic. The report found that executives are more likely to engage with traditional rather than non-traditional stakeholders. This is due to the risk of not meeting expectations, loss of control, not wasting time and damage to reputation. Implicit here is the need for more resources, extending well beyond the PR department, the resilience to manage the pressure and risks inherent, particularly when engaging with non-traditional stakeholders.

Not surprisingly the survey showed that trust, internal commitment, mutual respect, long-term focus and, yes, transparency are prerequisites of success. New media is seen as an important tool in achieving this. Interestingly stakeholder engagement came just below reputation management as the top priority, for chief communications officers (CCOs). So perhaps more research is needed on the link between the two. To many colleagues, stakeholder engagement was seen as a 'PR exercise', meaning it needs to become the responsibility of many managers, built into the cultural DNA, rather than simply a responsibility of the PR department. This implies that practitioners of this discipline need a wider range of skills, not least interpreting and advisory skills. However, the majority of interviewees thought it important 'to be in there shaping the debate about ourselves and our industry'. Given the lack of skills sets, appropriate structures and resources devoted to this process, it is not surprising that interviewees had the feeling of being overwhelmed by the sheer enormity of the task.

The Reputation Institute's 2013 Reputation Leaders' survey reported that 79 per cent of the 300 CEOs of global companies, plus their marketing and communications advisers, agreed that 'who you are matters more than what you produce'. Yet, worryingly, only 20 per cent believe their company is ready to compete, yet alone collaborate, in this new environment. There may have been some progress towards a more holistic response to stakeholder relations, yet few companies are prepared. Lack of a structured process and inability to leverage internal knowledge about stakeholder engagement were the factors cited. 'The fact is that when it comes to stakeholder relationship management, everything is *not* under control', the report concluded.

Just as there is a momentum towards integrated reporting, stakeholder integration is another key element of *Conscious Capitalism*, the title of a book by John Mackey and Raj Sisodia (2013). Their interpretation is that whereas traditional businesses treat their stakeholders (other than investors) as a means to achieving the goal of profit maximisation, 'conscious' businesses treat satisfying the needs of all major stakeholders as ends in themselves. 'Major' of course needs to be defined and this presupposes that stakeholders themselves agree with the company's prioritisation. The difference here being that if you seek trade-offs, you will always find them, yet if you look for synergies across the whole stakeholder spectrum, you can usually find those too. As Freeman (1984) wrote: 'Managing for stakeholders is not about zero-sum thinking, rather using innovation and entrepreneurship to make all key stakeholders better off.' This has the effect of lifting all boats rather than just the yachts.

Virtuous Circle

The stakeholder approach should be viewed as a virtuous circle, which starts with the company's purpose and values. This in turn serves to inspire the right team members, which leads to innovation and superior customer service, higher profits and eventually enhanced shareholder value. The metaphor of music and art to suggest creating harmony between stakeholders, rather than the typical analytical approach to individual stakeholders, thus ignoring the relationships between them is a good one.

To understand stakeholder relations, an additional kind of intelligence is required – systems intelligence (SQ), alongside emotional intelligence (EQ), and IQ. (This topic is covered in more detail elsewhere in the book.)

Some corporations, such as Shell and Nike, demonstrated that they have listened to and responded to their various internal and external stakeholders, including critics. At the same time NGOs such as WWF and Oxfam have adopted a more collaborative approach. This trend towards inclusiveness, partnership and dialogue has significant implications for methodologies and responsibilities entailed in stakeholder communication. One-way models of communication not only require intense efforts of coordination, but the question remains: Can companies 'control' particular meanings among and within stakeholder groups?

PR theory distinguishes between manipulation/persuasion and the more dialogic emphasis on education and facilitation of understanding. Dialogue is recommended as the best possible solution for the management of complex issues in the globalised world, what PR theorist Jim Grunig (1992) termed 'symmetrical two-way communication'. Yet, the concept of dialogue has been little examined in the stakeholder literature. Moreover, neither this literature nor that of PR considers the effects of language and culture. Nor do they mention their consequences for stakeholder identity and the potential risks of dialogue – notably 'cacophony', 'fragmentation' and 'paralysis'. This all goes to show that there may well be unintended consequences of stakeholder dialogue. These will need to be factored into the skills and mind-sets of business leaders, corporate cultures, strategies and structures, especially given the replacement of 'command and control' by 'collaboration and conversation'.

Preparing for any dialogue is as important as the dialogue process itself. This then feeds into the innovation and learning that different situations and contexts may throw up. In practice, much engagement is likely to be a mix of advocacy and dialogue. This is where the role of mediation becomes important. It is important that cultural knowledge is translated and shared across stakeholder groups. After all a strategic mind-set requires situational awareness and contextual intelligence.

Interdisciplinary Thinking

Our interpretation of these trends towards responsible stakeholder relationship building and maintenance is that much more interdisciplinary thinking will be required. It will require cooperation between the different management functions and alignment between theory and practice. In an age of sustainability, involving competitive conflict over natural resources (water, energy and food spring to mind), collaborative approaches are being chosen as alternatives to confrontation when solving complex social issues.

For example, Tata Companies take a holistic approach to bringing development to rural India. Finding methods to desalinate water, proving that literacy is not always a criterion for employment, helping communities to profit from traditional crafts and assisting in setting up self-help groups are some of the ways their subsidiaries try to add value. This is turn develops self-reliance among farmers. This is striking because India was ranked 93 out of 153 countries in the 2013 World Giving Index, yet was ranked fourth by Forbes for number of billionaires.

Unilever works with NGOs such as Oxfam to negotiate food-sourcing agreements with small-holding farmers in East Africa. As they deepen and widen engagement, the company is realising the need to be realistic about commitments, timescales and business models that are sustainable.

Collaboration

It is obvious that stakeholder engagement, involving collaborative approaches, allows companies to do business better, longer and more sustainably. It provides companies with tools to better address conflicts and articulate them before they arise, *integrating,* and that is the key word, different environmental, economic, social and public policy perspectives. This perspective helps companies make sustainable decisions. If only more companies would adopt it. Of course it does require quite an investment of time and budget. It is true that the need for sustainable development has fuelled the demand for wider participation in business decisions, well beyond the reach of most existing decision-making structures. Hence the growing role of multi-stakeholder problem-solving groups.

The CEO and the senior team are the trustees of these tasks which cannot be delegated to specialists, important as they are as advisers and implementers. One global company assigns a senior specialist to each member of senior management to assist with these interrelated tasks. If a company wants to change its mission, strategy and structures to accommodate what we are recommending, one of the most important prerequisites is to have a committed, engaged CEO. The World Economic Forum's Council on the Role of Business asks what measures can be taken to allow CEOs the job security to make short-term sacrifices for the sake of future gains – how can a culture of personal stewardship be instilled so that CEOs leave broader legacies and how can business schools play a role in promoting responsible mind-sets among business leaders, present and future? The World Economic Forum Council report in 2012 recommended that meaningful value considerations should be built into the corporate strategy, employee induction and promotion of senior management, including growing business leaders comfortable working across the private sector, government and civil society.

Renewing Leadership

Servant leaders thrive at this time of turbulence and complexity because they use their power to serve and develop others, tolerate ambiguity and adopt a 'systems view of the world', as Joe Jaworski (2012), an expert in transformational leadership describes it. But the author goes further than spiritual and emotional leadership by describing another level of leader called 'renewing leaders'. These kinds of leaders, in very short supply, embrace servant leadership but add visioning. This attempts to create the kind of society we desire by gaining a stronger awareness of the interconnectedness of life, via collaboration and joining the dots beyond narrow self-interest. In essence they have the sensitivity to negotiate between vested interest and societal interest.

Human Capitalism

As we have argued in the first chapter, in terms of the speed and reach of trends, new economies and 'glocalisation' are making a major difference, with new communities developing, linked not solely by geography or culture but by shared values, all magnified by social media.

Every year Asia House in London gives its business leader award to a CEO with servant leader qualities. In 2013 it went to an Indian Azim Premji, Chairman of WIPRO, who has also just been designated India's biggest philanthropist. This recognises those individuals who embody economic success and professional excellence combined with moral leadership. This is not a bad summary of what we mean and what is required to take on stakeholder engagement initiatives that add economic and social value.

Stakeholder primacy is the way for global business to engage and connect with people at a deeper level, by integrating dialogue and diplomacy, reputation and relationships with responsible leadership.

Summary

1. Business should remain the key driver of wealth creation but needs to reframe the narrative to embrace the broader socio/cultural and sustainability context. The 'triple bottom line' of economics, ethics and environment are equally important and mutually interdependent.

2. Reshaping the future requires a broader leadership on the part of business, sensitive to a broader ecosystem of relationships, but needs to be empowered to provide personal stewardship and longer-term thinking. This has implications for government regulation and corporate governance structures. Replacing transactions with relationships inevitably leads to a longer-term orientation.

3. Balancing the shareholder with the stakeholder approach is win–win and the only way to progress. Yet stakeholder dialogue needs to be put on a more strategic and inclusive footing if it is to be sustainable. There are risks, but they should be seen as opportunities for learning and building new thinking across the whole supply chain.

4. Build into the knowledge management system inputs and influences from not just economic and market analysis, but those of a cultural, psychological and relational nature. This has implications for recruitment, training and education as well as corporate culture.

5. The use of more unified reporting strategies, embracing the commercial and environmental/social elements, would not only aid transparency but lead to greater trust, a vital factor in this challenging and uncertain world.

PART III
Shaping Stakeholder Strategies

Chapter 4
Global Urbanisation and Social Change

In Chapters 1, 2 and 3 we established a coherent theme, which underpins every argument in the book. We have established the rather obvious, but frequently missed, importance of leadership before any other change. The use of the phrase 'Leadership Landscape' as part of the title of this book refers to the importance of accepting the wider horizon. Business leadership operates within global parameters and should not be considered as only a narrow functional process untouched by societal pressure. Wider corporate and business demands will increasingly maintain powerful bottom line requirements not to mention the need to adhere in cultural terms to the ethical priniciples discussed earlier in Chapter 2. Such ethical standards will increasingly refer in the decade ahead to interactive relationships with all stakeholders and the wider socio-business environment.

As we gaze into the future, the actions leaders must take to meet the positive objectives discussed relate to the wider ethics of eco-sustainability. None of the standards set in the coming decades are passing fancies. They consist of evolving relationships that will be increasingly demanded by populations in every part of the world and may well play an important part in business to business and consumer demand as well as forming an important part of every company's external reputation (see Chapter 6). We cannot refer to each decision-making strategy as if they are separate functions: 'get it right and all will be well'. In some instances this may be the case, but in this book we are concerned with macro change, not the micro decisions standing alone influenced only by external change. In the forthcoming chapters we argue that every change is affected by a mountain range of massive but different influences. One such pressure may pass unnoticed at first by the people most affected. One example may well be the overwhelming yet long-term influence of urbanisation. We have used this word as our chapter title but it is not totally accurate for the reasons above. The tractions for changes of this magnitude have no single cause – they follow a combination and range of different market forces, government policies and geopolitical policies.

By the year 2050, when current business leaders and stakeholder communities will know how many of our forecasts have become reality, the UN expects the global number of city dwellers to reach 6.3 billion. Or, put another way, there will be almost as many people living in urban environments as today's *total* world population of seven billion. We are living through a period of fast urbanisation. In comparative terms it is as great as the move from the farmlands of nineteenth-century England to the new industrialised cities being built like Manchester, Birmingham, Sheffield, Newcastle, Leeds and many others.

In this chapter we develop the argument that in the decade ahead even minor changes will impact business and NGO leaders. Managers and organisation leaders will only succeed if they become closely involved in the global community and refuse to be onlookers. Business managers, whatever their product or service, must widen their gaze and, in doing so, realise attitudes which shape the opinions of their publics are themselves being shaped globally. Online media with blog feeds into websites are being read by the very people a chief executive wants to influence to buy products or ideas. The same philosophy exists for patrons of charities or campaigners trying to change public opinion.

Urban Change Impacts Individuals

Business leaders and politicians in particular often fail to appreciate the fundamental changes that societal groupings have on transmission and understanding of interpersonal communications, verbal, written or online.

For example, a social group of middle-class consumers talking at a gathering in the Australian outback or a village in India may exchange ideas and views in their conversations. Their discussion will differ from a similar social group in an urban venue but, by the content, vocabulary and style of phraseology, they could be speaking a different language, even if the tongue is the same. The social cues and references, the range of abstract words used and the size of the vocabularies will be significantly varied. It is accepted by journalists that readers of a popular tabloid newspaper use perhaps 10 per cent of the number of different words employed in a more upmarket broadsheet. But differences can be more fundamental as we apply what is termed 'discourse analysis'. This brings to the fore different pressures and influences unconsciously accepted from parents, grandparents, education levels and content affecting the way the message is transmitted and received.

It is for this reason we have included in this chapter an emphasis on physical changes that are frequently wrought by the urban process and the importance of the cultural invasion that accompanies such physical change. These elements influence the style, content and systems that come into play during what we have described as the impact of stakeholder interaction. Equally important is the leadership factor. Museums, art galleries and literature do not come into existence on their own. Business and political leadership sets the scene and provides the fertile ground.

The impact on people's thinking and the societal changes which took place in nineteenth-century England were dramatic. It affected the population in so many ways, of which possessing watches and clocks because factories demanded punctuality was only one of the more obvious changes in lifestyles and communications.

Academics such as Professor Ricky Burdett of the London School of Economics (LSE) is quoted in *The Economist* (2013a), as saying integrated systems for collecting, processing and acting on data offers the equivalent in terms of impact of a 'second electrification' within new smart cities. He suggests that the power cables which transformed nineteenth-century urbanisation so that it was able to supply electricity for the massive buildings then being erected, control their sewage and later the underground transport to support them, changed the intercommunication processes of the urban population. The ability to travel easily and quickly changes urban habits, employment opportunities and social life.

Today the effect of population change may not seem as dramatic as in the nineteenth century. For business leaders affected by the thinking we forecast, today's changes will be equally significant. The shift from industrial society to an information society has already had its impact on macro attitudes in the community. Graham and Marvin summed it up in their book *Splintering Urbanism* (2001) when they said the contemporary process of ideological and technological change, accompanied by market and economic forces in parallel with political action, have together generated a splintering of urban life, which at times was anti-democratic. The importance of the right university degrees and an ability to articulate clearly in what we term 'a leadership style' is still related to education and parental influence. It is currently even more intense and more precisely directed than it was in the post-Second World War period where the influence of the 1930s continued to overlap despite the end of wartime hostilities.

The Rapidity of Urban Change

Many sociologists talk about 'network change' which strictly refers to people relationships but, because they see and record physical functions, they group such changes under the one heading. This means network change now refers also to transport, telecommunications, buildings for community meetings and the impact of lavishly built retail venues. The last, of course, soon develop as shopping malls, which provide pleasurable centres for community relationship, which grow organically to become self-generating networks. In addition, the changes include and become involved in transport services, home delivery systems, and support services such as post offices, estate agents and bureaux for accommodation. The list is endless. The urban phenomenon grows exponentially and many of the changes require continuous effort by government leaders at local and national level to sustain their function. The intensity and speed of these changes stimulates discourse. Research on higher primates suggests the more intensive the social grouping the more rapid the intellectual development. We believe such theses apply to homo sapiens also.

Capitalism to work at its full capacity needs movement of offices, people and the circulation of money through financial institutions such as banks. When the support services are in place and the regulations properly updated, monitored and policed, there is a framework within which free enterprise can operate. Modern societies comprise a complexity of human resources that must be free to utilise various levels of knowledge and education that attract more people services from the junior staff, trainees up to the management escalator at boardroom-level with its specialised infrastructure. Each level of staff needs its own service support from cloud data to infra-company telecommunications that moves data from internal audiences to the external without a hitch. In such a process, a global circulation system for multichannel information generates its own traction. In some ways it even unveils visual screens through the built environment. The new smart city projects generate their own employment opportunities because qualified staff want to work in such carefully designed environments.

Primary and Secondary Networking

From families and close friends gossiping about their locality, personalised networks have grown to a sophisticated level of social and business relationships organised on a systematic basis. There is a steady generation of concentric rings – what could be termed primary and secondary opinion leadership.

There was a time, now past, when the parish priest passed on news and information from nearby towns and villages. The urban dweller is today, however, overwhelmed by information from local and national media, television and online Google sourcing. As the LSE sociologist Richard Sennett maintains, the urban smart city dweller is under increasing pressure from a cascade of views, opinions and the generation of intensive attention directed at them personally and at their workplace. Such daily attacks can emanate from anyone with a PC or laptop computer. Many corporate directors of public affairs are already recoiling from the attention of small pressure groups who are as sophisticated in their communications skills for projecting messages and the use of media support as the professionals working for small organisations.

The larger companies worry less. They have the budgets and intellectual support needed to respond and possibly resist most pressure groups.

Jane Jacobs, in her bestselling book *The Death and Life of Great American Cities* (1961), argues that 'cities have the capability of providing something for everybody, only because, and only when, they are created by everybody'.

She is a celebrated American–Canadian journalist, author and activist whose seminal work is often cited for slowing the urban redevelopment of Toronto. She describes the dangers that can occur during urban renewal programmes, which she considers to be psychologically violent and destructive because they destroy many of the legitimate community organisations. She argues that such programmes can create unnatural urban spaces which encourage intellectual voids that can be filled by any small well-organised pressure group directing their attack on local authority decision makers or, in the case of business interests, commercial involvements that could be to the advantage of the wider community. She advocates 'four generators of diversity', which in combination create effective economic pools of use. These conditions consist of: mixed usages that will activate streets at different times of the day, small blocks or areas that encourage pedestrian movement, varied buildings of various ages and design stimulating pedestrian interest with moderate levels of density.

Jacobs frequently cites New York City's Greenwich Village as an example of a vibrant urban community. Greenwich Village, like many similar communities, has been preserved at least in part by her writing and activism. Her book played a major role in slowing the urban redevelopment of Toronto in Canada, where she was involved in the campaign to stop the Spadina Expressway. The Wikipedia description says that her writing is sometimes adduced as an important influence on New Urbanism, architecture and the planning movements that emerged in the 1980s, but which can be seen as at odds with her idea of the layered, spontaneous, multi-ethnic, multi-income level, non-gated authentic community.

Sometimes there is an intensity of action by very small groups who operate as a single theme or message organisation. They often appear to be highly democratic while actually representing no more than a handful of people such as one street or building block. The author (RW) has experience in local community situations where high-sounding bodies are no more than small groups who have registered themselves with an important sounding title. When RW was an elected local authority councillor in central London, one small electoral area had 32 such organisations. Such small informal groups play an important part in the stimulation of the stakeholder concept with organisations on this micro-scale and should not be ignored. It is important to recognise and identify such small groups and realise the stakeholder concepts and methodologies we describe here are as effective in small community groups as they are within large-scale multinationals.

Are Developers Really as People-oriented as They Profess?

The problem senior managers will face in the decade ahead is that the developers who generate the built environment within which the new urban dwellers will enter and build their own community are more concerned about the profitable use of new building technologies than they are about the people who will live in them. They will discover how builders concentrate on the new technologies available rather than delve more deeply into the psychological impact of the buildings on workers and inhabitants. As one world famous architect commented at a lecture this author (RW) attended: 'I will not be remembered for my creativity but because my buildings don't leak.' The comment was an amusing swing at one of the massive developments in the City of London beset by maintenance problems at that time.

The Smart City

As we gaze forward, aspiring leaders of organisations should be aware of the direction in which smart cites will move. A paragraph in *The Economist's* article 'Cities: The Multiplexed Metropolis' (*The Economist*, 2013a) describes this situation. It suggests that engineers were already dreaming of a digital nervous system for cities that captured, for example, how many windows have lights turned on behind them. From such data, powerful computers will do the crunch, optimise the overall operation and tell the authorities about incipient problems. 'Unlocking a one trillion dollar opportunity' was the tagline of a 'smart city' workshop earlier in 2013. *The Economist* feature went on to suggest that, with the right tools hooked up, it would allow a new level of integrated response. A fire alarm would not simply call out the fire engine, it would determine their best route, redirect traffic away from it, warn schools to close windows and make sure there were no nearby water mains shut down for maintenance. Big events could be predicted and planned for. The article suggested that some of the new big cities could aspire to having a Chief Information Officer whose system would be able to spot things like free parking spaces, queues in front of museums, full rubbish bins and even suspicious movements of people. Many of these planned smart cities could aspire to having a NASA-type control room where teams of operators monitored cameras around the city.

The need for a functioning public transport system to support the retail needs of the incoming migrant has already been mentioned. As the prosperity of migrants grow, personalised transport also expands in tune with that growth. Sadly the evidence of most global cities is that strategic planning timetables for automobile movements usually fall well behind need. Whether the reference is New York, London or any other vibrant city with a historic past, traffic jams and transport difficulties are the norm. In so many cases the obvious choice of road tunnels and bridges are realised too late. For economic reasons the solutions become so difficult, if not dramatic, in their consequences for the built environment that the solutions, which should have been in place at an earlier stage, are tied to the second line 'over building'. Because of this the potential decision by local planners for signing off the solution is deferred. Logjams of traffic intensify the public debate so that solutions become less likely to occur until it is too late. In some cities such as Los Angeles and Sydney, where space is at less of a premium, the road systems are adequate for the traffic movement but not adequate for all levels of immigrant demand by residents wanting a modern culture that can grow like 'Barbarians at the Gate' and add even more to the pressure on business leaders to become involved. The strategic timeframe for many built environments differ by years from likely responses to political and governmental policies that might have helped residents lives in terms of easier transportation and movement.

One country that has met the problem of city overcrowding, because of its size and open spaces, is India. Mumbai is so overcrowded that traffic movement is choked, due to a massive immigrant influx. With 20 million people living in the city, rents are soaring as the glamour of their film industry and exciting high-tech projects attract what we call a visible personification of the market place as a magnet for creative younger generations (similar in many ways to London's attractions). Mumbai is now creating a second overspill development; such is the pressure on city government. When one of their government ministers remarked, only partly joking, that the city needed more toilets than temples, it caused a political furore. Yet this is the type of imbalance that occurs when countries struggle too quickly to catch up on the economic rat race. Fortunately India has the space and genuinely creative entrepreneurs and, providing they are given the freedom, will drive forward with the vision needed to strengthen what we have called the 'market magnet'. Karnataka is an area in India that contains the massive Electronic City spread over 350 acres. It is the brainchild of the first chairman of Karnatara Electronics who had the vision of building a Silicon Valley in India, a country which now has a 10,000 kilometre expressway on an elevated highway, the longest in the country. This is yet another example of where informed and creative leadership can play such an important role in the new society we envisage, if given the opportunity by national and local government.

The contrast between the situation in India, where political structures are establishing a democratic process, and a wealthy nation state such as Abu Dhabi are marked. Thanks to the established system and the wealth to provide the traction, Abu Dhabi has taken the longer government-led methodology to create a societal and economic brand. It takes the formation of a powerful long-term Urban Structural Framework to optimise city development through a plan that takes them into 2030. It needed a next generation mind-set controlling an Urban Planning Council that can obviously avoid many of India's mistakes because Abu Dhabi is small, wealthier and possibly pays less attention to what the Western nations would consider to be an over-zealous democratic system.

Despite the impressive town planning of Abu Dhabi, it is significant that even the quality of their forward thinking has made them realise there are concepts and themes they can learn from one other global cities, and possibly the most impressive of them all, Singapore. It is a city–state that has been described by the Israeli/Canadian architect, urban designer and theorist Moshe Safdie (author of the seminal book *Beyond Habitat*, 1973) as 'the most cutting edge city in the world. They have very effective guidelines for development and they review design as they evolve'.

It has an Urban Redevelopment Authority (URA) which prepares long-term plans as well as local area plans driven by the physical land restraints. Planning in Singapore has guided its physical development from the day this city–state was founded in 1819 by Sir Stamford Raffles, who had to solve the need for a harbour to service the whole of the Southeast Asia. From that time forward it realised its importance as the entrepôt centre, which could, and did, compete with Hong Kong.

In the decades ahead, and with the growing identification of more small groups of residents capable of making their views known and demanding replies, the new designs for individual transport products will keep changing the strategic demand for new planning ideas. For example, the automobile industry will be launching new transport systems that can make elements in planning development redundant. Electric cars are a case in point. When battery weights are reduced and self-driving cars without drivers will probably enable high concentrations of individual cars per square metre, they could reduce demand for some elements in the highway system, not to mention traffic furniture. This could produce an immediate demand for better road systems such as tunnels and fast moving freeways. Changes to detailed design may dramatically alter the wider planning needs of the surrounding region. Legislation and public acceptance of the changes to vehicle design could pose a range of influences on the technologies for car-to-car communications that will need to be overcome. Ian Robertson, BMW's Head of European Sales is quoted as saying (*Financial Times*, 2013d): that vehicle technologies 'have the potential to push the industry further forward in the next five years than it has in the past 100.' Such changes may appear irrelevant but they form a significant part of urban change and the societal influences that will follow. Changes at even a micro level need a quick leadership response and to be understood in the cascade of acceptability by every level of management.

Local Government

Every one of the advances and technological developments mentioned will be determined by different levels of leadership at a local, regional and national government level. Stakeholder decisions and their consequent communication programmes become important at these national and local levels. It will become necessary for leaders in business and non-profit organisations to also understand the complexities and working methods of local government as national governments morph more of their powers down to local bodies. This author (RW) spent 20 years in two timeframes of ten years each as an elected representative on one East Anglian (South East UK) Authority and another on the Council of the City of Westminster in London. In such roles this author was able, as a leader, to create planned housing areas where older property was brought up to date, regular residents and local official relationships evolved, and such areas integrated into more modern standard building.

In the UK it is normal for an elected councillor to maintain their careers in parallel. This is even maintained when they hold executive positions within their town or city council. The contrast between local authority management and that of management within a business environment is stark but external audiences and electors as interest groups seldom realise these differences. The interrelation between elected management decision making and other such local government functions can be dependent on the quality of the elected representatives, the local government officials and their relationships in terms of each understanding the others agendas. In future, local officials should be made aware of their own stakeholder constituency. In such cases the electorate is a primary stakeholder but on secondary levels other officials from different departments constitute stakeholders, as does local businesses and charitable organisations.

The leaders of city and town councils will, if trained as managers, ensure there is an efficient stakeholder process, but the need for more formalised procedures is a lacuna waiting to be filled, perhaps at national government level in the UK and in other countries. It is a subject frequently under discussion by those involved in public life.

To help readers not familiar with the London, UK local government system it may be helpful at this stage to explain its rather complex system. This description is included because there reaches a stage where a city is of such a size that it almost becomes a city–state. In such situations the stakeholder process as discussed in this book takes on a significant role in the leadership decision process.

It is perhaps strange that London, one of the largest and most successful cities in the world, has a system so complex that few of its inhabitants understand it nor could they explain even its basic structure if stopped in what New York market researchers would define a 'mall intercept'. The reason for London's government complexity is historic and suffers from a selection of changes through the last thousand years when perhaps the most sensible policy would have been to scrap the whole system and start again. We will avoid over-complicated historic references to the fact the city, under Roman occupation from 55BC to approximately 400AD and called then Londinium, is formally titled today 'The City of London' as if it applied to the whole city.

In subsequent years, the City has spread Westwards, engulfing an area nearly 20 miles in diameter, involving many boroughs which started out life as villages but are now well-established London suburbs but still designated with a London postal district code. This, like most large cities, can cause confusion with what appears to be a double name. An example might be: Putney, London, SW15. This code then has letters and figures to identify the actual road or house position within that road. The postal code is useful data for business and trade deliveries anxious to find a residence or venue quickly and for the development of marketing strategies.

The government of London as a large city is more difficult to understand because there is a City of London and a City of Westminster, with many boroughs both within Westminster and also outside the two cities, constituting suburbs but still carrying London postal codes.

There is an elected Mayor of London who has strategic decision-making powers with selected direct control of the Metropolitan Police, security, fire services, sport and some cultural activity maintained broadly by a number of Deputy Mayors. For historical reasons the City of London has its own Lord Mayor elected annually by its councillors who are themselves elected by the small number of residents in the City of London and commercial institutions. The Lord Mayor of the City of London has no direct decision-making power but, in full historic regalia, travels around the world representing the City of London and promoting its financial services.

The centre of London, rather like Manhattan in New York, is the City of Westminster and also has a Lord Mayor and Deputy Lord Mayor selected by elected councillors, whose Leader of the majority political party has decision-making powers over the management of the City of Westminster. The normal practice in the UK is for the management of cities and boroughs to be maintained by the 'Leader' of the majority party but more recently some cities have moved towards an elected Mayor with decision-making powers of management. In London there is one exception, Newham, a borough which has now appointed an elected Mayor with full decision-making power within its border. This is unusual but the concept has gathered momentum as it is seen as an advantage over the normal system where the Mayor being independent has no political association but represents the borough at formal events.

Business and other organisational leaders should carry out detailed research on the current political or quasi-political policy thinking before making direct approaches on behalf of stakeholders.

The global arguments as to whether towns and cities are better governed by directly elected Mayors or the system where Mayors are primarily ceremonial, with the government and decision making carried out by the Leader of the majority political party, constitutes an on-going debate. The advantage of the UK system is that the Mayor is a neutral head of the town or city even if devoid of actual power. Rather as the British Monarch, although the head of state is clearly ceremonial, also has considerable influence because of their non-political status. Because the Monarch has gained international knowledge and understanding during their reign, and they also have weekly private meetings with the country's Prime Minister, their influence is powerful, as can be said of many Lord Mayors in their respective cities.

During the last decade a number of cities in the UK have moved to directly elected Mayors with decision-making functions. Time will provide notice and perhaps financial data as to whether tasting the pudding in London and other cities will prove the argument one way or the other. It is too early to decide at this stage which is the more efficient. In France it has been a normal process for many years, but directly elected Mayors for small and medium-sized towns are not the same as directly elected Mayors with full decision-making powers in cities of many million populations. The French system, where Chambers of Commerce in small towns performs a function that is not restricted to business interactions alone and work closely with the local Mayor to ensure the business community gains from the local authority's decision making has proved a valuable asset for their respective towns.

Benjamin Barber, a Senior Research Scholar at the City University of New York, argues the case in his book *If Mayors Ruled the World: Dysfunctional Nations, Rising Cities* (2013) for increased powers to be placed in the hands of directly elected Mayors with full managerial power. He argues his case with great fervour and many of his arguments regarding the importance of the locally based decision-making process are accepted by those actively involved. Certainly the need to establish stakeholder communications would improve the efficiency of the leader or elected Mayor, but anyone who has been actively involved in the process of local authority decision making will know that what sounds like effective government when described in the Platonic terms of ancient Greece will know that modern urban living is complex with many varied interests, the actualities of which can be very different. Democracy, as believed in ancient Greece with citizens arguing in the market place, is no template for modern towns with their online communications and professional pressure groups forcing a vote even before the debate has run its course.

A simple request by a group of residents for example, or indeed a single resident, to obtain permission for a building extension to their house or a change in the development of a road, can result in many and varied objections by neighbours. Even a small application to a building can still take many hours of discussion and frequently needs repeated committee meetings as the UK's democratic system winds its way slowly towards an end which hopefully will satisfy the majority of people in the community.

As this author (RW) has sat as a member of many town planning committees both in and outside London, he could surprise Benjamin Barber by the many times planning committees have to meet to arrive at even the simplest solution. Even after hours of discussion the ire of non-participating residents will still be aroused in many parts of the community who will express their views vehemently in the correspondence columns of the local media. The strength of the democratic system over the totalitarian process that can be the result of systems where the Mayor has total decision-making powers is that decision makers have to achieve a common acceptance otherwise they fail to get elected next time. That is the strength of the democratic system. It is not just about having general elections, which in many ways elect a dictatorial authority for a parliamentary term. The real effect of democracy is at the grassroots where the officials and elected representatives, some national and some local, know their jobs are on the line if they upset or fail to appreciate the needs of each elector. Such attitudes are seldom apparent in totalitarian regimes.

The success of China's massive redevelopment projects have taken place because buildings that stand in the way were removed regardless of the financial interests of residents living on the sites. The apparently long-winded process of the British local government system compared to that of, say France, is because the democratic process at local level requires a lengthier period of discussion in an attempt to be fair to everyone involved. In the majority of cases the solutions are acceptable, even if patience may be exhausted in the process.

City Networking

For business and political leaders the human element of networking must not be marginalised. The operation is significant as the elements of urbanisation evolve through many stages, which correlate with physical change. Even today in modestly sized towns and cities, a resident moving home from one district to another quickly realises there are differences in the networking or friend-making structures among resident groups. The residents may not realise they are indulging in what sociologists call 'networking', but that is what it is. They are urban dwellers and the physical structure throws people closely together creating a climate for personal interaction. Such groups have access to their local authority where officials identify problems despite the political implications that may influence the final decision. A group of residents organised into, say the Acacia Avenue Residents Association, becomes an informal pressure group ready to demand the presence at their meetings of local officials representing the town's government, possibly a police officer and fireman, or whoever can right a believed wrong for that group. Such relationships can be a starting point for a formalised stakeholder communication where transference of opinions and messages on their own is not enough. Residents increasingly demand a role in the decision-making process. The methodologies suggested here for business stakeholder relationships need to be applied by local and national government officials, just as they are being increasingly accepted within the business community.

On a more macro level the community institutions and associations can, on a regional level, generate secondary groups of interest who may also bring pressure to bear on businesses, charities, or any other organisation. We use the phrase 'pressure group' because that is what informally they are, although few of their members would consider themselves part of an organised pressure group.

Examples such as Chambers of Commerce, local branches of professional bodies – in the UK – the Institute of Directors, the Confederation of British Industry (CBI) or indeed legal, accountancy, marketing and PR professional bodies, all maintain local systems of elected representatives, many of which attract what sociologists call 'joiners'. Political parties each have their own local and regional associations who not only perform the duties of organising social events to raise funds, but also select candidates for higher office such as the local authority, the national Parliament or European Parliament. Depending on the political colour of the district and thus its representatives it will respond to the relationship-building techniques of business and organisational pressure.

The final paragraph of the previously quoted *Economist* article (2013a) says:

> *The balance between what a city provides and what is sorted out by its citizens and the companies they do business with will differ from place to place. That variety should, in itself, act as a safeguard against dystopia. One of the great elements of city life is they can and do compete with each other. In most countries people have at least some choice as*

to which city to live and do business in. The quality of the information
platform a city offers will increasingly become a factor in those choices.
Future cities may seek to control their internal flows of goods, services
and even citizens. They will not be able to stop a run for the exits.

Detroit is an example of a city, once dominant in its field of auto manufacture, that recently filed in the US for bankruptcy protection after some years of decline. To understand that creative thinking about urbanisation is a crucial factor for businesses and their relationships with the environment within which they operate, it is important to understand and relate to the human person. In the case of Detroit, their local government looked to the Federal Government to help them respond to their $18 billion worth of debt. When the motor industry showed signs of difficulty in that state they were met with considerable financial support but they actually needed the type of new thinking that many of the industrial areas in the North East of England generated when the coal mining and heavy metal industries suffered terminal decline from market changes and competition in the late twentieth century.

Today, visitors to the Newcastle/Sunderland and Gateshead conurbations in the North East of the UK see a thriving region of creative technological services interacting with academia and cultural events that draw people from all over the country. Like so many successful towns globally there is a powerful interaction between universities and the surrounding business and support systems. Regions change, although continuing over more than a decade they often fulfil the criteria laid out by Bartlett Professor of Planning at University College London, Sir Peter Hall, in his book *Good Cities, Better Lives* (2013). There are 'five basic challenges faced by modern cities of rebalancing the urban economies, linking people and places through integrated land use and transport planning, living with finite resources and fixing the broken machinery so as to bring public and private agencies together in the process of development and redevelopment'. These issues must be addressed, he says, if we are to acquire the lost art of urbanism. He goes on to say there is a vital role universities can play in the regeneration of their home cities and not just through the development of technology parks. He considers economic growth comes from investment in linking university and other research to the creation of attractive modern urban environments and that planners should recast universities to make them agents of technical and cultural change.

Business schools are frequently one of the first academic institutions along with engineering faculties to follow in the wake of urban expansion. In the last century, countries like India saw a rapid expansion to their economies with forecasters claiming it would be a close run thing as to whether China or India took world leadership in terms of economic growth over the next 20 years. The country has a young population with none of the restrictions on family size that we see generating demographic imbalances in China. In India the expansion created a powerful middle class which, combined with a free flow of investment capital, generated a plethora of business schools that would hopefully underpin expected demand. As Ajit Rangnekar, Dean of the Indian School of Business said in the *Financial Times* (2013b): 'A whole lot of opportunists and some charlatans started all sorts of business schools thinking this is the magic mantra for making money.' Sadly, with something of a downturn later in the Indian economy, many of the smaller, less quality-driven business schools have suffered with more than 160 shutting down since 2011. Even so, as Amit Garga of the Parthenon Consulting Group says (*Financial Times*, 2013b): 'You can make a return on equity of 30 per cent to 35 per cent.' Despite the economic downturn, the number of management schools in India doubled between 2008 and 2012 to 2,385 and the student intake in 2013 was up from 114,803 to 313,920. These figures speak for themselves when seen in the context of expanding urbanisation. Student numbers of this size can do nothing but impact the cultural and educational life of newly expanding cities. The All India Council for Technical Education, which is the statutory body for accreditation, considers there are now 400,000 seats at management schools across India, but as many as one in eight remain empty each year, forcing some of the less profitable schools to close. There is a significant demand in India for higher education, but there is a demand gap for quality.

It should be noticed that many of the world economies have put the building of universities at the top of their priority lists, arguing they should take a leading roles in the expansion of their economies. According to the *The Times* Higher Education Rankings for 2014, even President Vladimir Putin has decreed that five Russian universities must feature among the world's top 100 by 2020 and 100,000 Brazilian students will join the world's leading institutions, backed by generous scholarships. *The Times* article does make some provisos that in 2013 only five institutions from emerging economies appeared in the World University Ranking 2013 top 200. It stresses that emerging economies are at different stages of their journey and there is some way to go before their efforts reach fruition. The overall ranking remains heavily dominated by North America and Western Europe, despite the ravages of austerity.

These issues provide an important example of the range of responses, some good, some bad that can occur following urbanisation. Once the initial phases are past a period of consolidation can follow, but even then government controls need to be maintained. In the UK there has been a Government initiative to free up appropriate education institutions and to encourage easier links between qualifications managed by professional bodies and university accreditation. Already some concerns are being expressed by the *Times Higher Education* that rigorous standards must be maintained.

The counter problem to the cultural advantages of a university presence in any city is the basic need for low-cost accommodation. A headline in the *Financial Times* (2013c) 'No Room for Graduates in Central London as Rents Soar out of Reach' sums up that particular problem. London, a large city, has eight universities and even a small city such as Leeds in the North of England has three. When the balance is maintained between size and demand there are many interpersonal factors seldom recorded or even fully understood. The same article (*Financial Times*, 2013c) had a secondary heading: 'How the Property Hothouse Forces Relationships'. One student interviewed commented that when he moved into a flat with his girlfriend the motivation was because of the need to avoid high rents to be paid on his own. As he said, living in London forces you to have uncomfortable living arrangements with people you do not know and it is frequently difficult to move out. On the other hand, some people stay in a shared property longer than they would otherwise because they cannot afford a one-bedroom apartment. However, research has shown that in thriving international cities six out of ten people tend to be graduates, either under or post graduate. Such pressures form a normal but frequent element of societal change, all of which can play a role in social decision making as one part of various stakeholder processes.

The impact of global cultural activity is one of the signposts of change that will continue its forward surge in the coming decades. New York has been an example where it neared bankruptcy in the 1970s but the decade of the oil crisis was the traction behind an 'artistic explosion', which spread across blocks of the city which hitherto had been seen as almost too dangerous to inhabit. Cultural explosions mean more than visual artists taking studios alongside each other, where they frequently utilise the walls of nearby restaurants to sell their art work.

The building of art museums is reaching epidemic proportions in medium to large urban towns and boroughs. The creation of cultural infrastructures can sometimes lead and sometimes follow public demand. The new urban leadership, whether it is government derived or sponsored by the new business groups, will depend on enlightened leadership. As a Special Report by *The Economist* (2013f) comments:

Museums used to stand for something old, dusty, boring and barely relevant to real life … the more successful ones have changed out of all recognition. The range they cover has broadened spectacularly and now goes well beyond subjects such as art and artefacts science and history … they have also become pits of popular debate and places where children want to go. Places where they look and learn.

These changes must be driven by an interactive relationship between cultural leaders, financial support from business and from sympathetic governments.

In 2012 American museums received $850 million. That is more than all the big league sporting events and theme parks combined. In England over half the adult population visited a museum or gallery in the previous year. In Sweden three out or four go to a museum at least once a year. China will soon have 4,000 museums and is racing to catch up with the US which has over four times that many.

Developed countries are being championed by a wide variety of interest groups, city fathers, who see iconic buildings and great collections as a tourist draw, and urban planners who regard museums as a magic wand to bring blighted city areas back to life. The cultural plethora, whether it is a museum or a theatre, provides vehicles for population networking and stakeholder relations.

Managing Complexity

For the business and organisational leader in the new environment, the challenge is to manage complexity. In the past when letters and reports could take months to arrive at their destination, managers now operate in real time with information and data crunched in seconds with responses sent back to the sender the same morning. Decisions have to be made immediately. For the entrepreneur and owner–manager this does not pose a problem unless they multitask across serial stakeholders. For world-class global institutions, layered decision making cannot be tolerated.

As Don Tapscott, author of *Wikinomics: Four Principles of the Open World* (2012) comments: 'The information revolution is replacing one kind of management: command and control with another based on self-organising networks.' As one speaker commented at an international conference in 2013, there is a 'growing disconnect between linear institutions and the non-linear world'. Many of the world's largest companies thrive on simplicity by concentrating on simple niche products where they aim for dominance in that market. As reported in *The Economist* (2013d): 'Coca-Cola are masters of distilling their corporate identity into a simple formula which employees can internalise and customers can easily recognise'.

McDonald's is a global success because its business model is so simple and replicable. Tim Brown, the boss of design house IDEO, argues that design companies like his are enjoying success by showing organisations 'how to design complexity out'. It could be argued that the conglomerates of the 1960s crumbled because they tried to manage too many businesses in too many different industries.

It is only when the cities generate wealth-creating businesses that cultural expansion feeds on itself. In London, the creative graduates from universities and art schools became the driving force behind cultural activities through pop, classical music and design. Ultimately the expansion of many design consultancies to a size and significance where they can argue that visual design represents their clients' underlying identity is a dangerous crossover of disciplines. It tends to imply that if a bridge design looks good it must also be strong in engineering terms. From small beginnings as art centres within run-down urban areas, these small service industries followed the Silicon Valley example and built significant businesses with global products, creating corporate graphic images embraced by Fortune 500 companies. The design houses became and have become global operations themselves with offices across the world. There has been a re-examination of traditional architecture and, more importantly, the election of local government councillors and specialist expert representatives sitting on town planning committees who were themselves products of the cultural volcano.

Culture in the Driving Seat

A stroll on Sunday afternoon in New York through the Lower East Side and Chelsea West Side, which is home to more than a hundred art galleries, from West 14th to West 26th Streets means wealthy 'suits' will metaphorically meet and address other wealthy figures who are normally at home on weekdays in Wall Street. The phenomenon is less apparent in London because cultural activity is more widely spread but the same trend of what marketing specialists would call the 'top end' of the socio-economic strata gathers and uses its buying power through involvement with bodies such as the Contemporary Art Society. Founded in 1910 by wealthy patron Lady Ottoline Morrell and artist Roger Fry to 'educate the philistine English', the Contemporary Art Society now has a large and influential membership, buying modern art for distribution to regional galleries. Art and culture in its widest form, which includes music, literature and theatre, has become an accepted vehicle for rebuilding urban areas integrated often with technology and what is frequently termed the Silicon Valley Effect. These are not artificial or fashionable influences on urbanisation but an environment or set of mores where business leaders can integrate personally into their own vision of close stakeholder relationships.

Of course there will be economic ups and downs. Most business people have experienced the best and the worst. Sadly the influence of the specialist media on business thinking has intensified as business and organisational activities have increased exponentially. Sadly that expansion has in many ways removed the direct influence of expert colleagues as individuals on each other. The pavement as office, which existed in the concentrated financial quarters in the City of London and Wall Street during the earlier part of the last century, no longer exists. Walking from the office at lunchtime in the financial City of London square mile was an interactive process. Bank rate changes, possible takeover bids and economic trends were discussed and company results considered as financial managers met casually in the street. The discussion was intensified by others who joined the discussion in the small restaurants where club-like atmospheres existed. The small, almost backroom, restaurants in narrow back alleys and streets had remained for 200 years, but are now struggling to compete with the invasion of international coffee shop chains. The change of venue style alters the customer and intercommunicative changes along with its verbal content and cues, and widens discourse.

'Being in the City' meant investment knowledge was ahead of the game nationally. Despite there being three evening newspapers in the City of London in the 1950s, suburban private investors or small companies were just behind the times in terms of being able to respond quickly and take action. Online communications has taken over that rapid exchange of information within most countries although globally such exchanges, because of time differences, can still result in short time lags for the print and electronic media such as television despite a marginal levelling effect in terms of time synchronisation. The effect of this has not always been helpful for business managers. Opinions by journalists interpreting changes in economic or fiscal data, frequently exaggerate in their writing the significance of statistical changes even when writing in the traditional media. Drama still drives even the broadsheets. Marketing policies exert their pressure there as indeed they do in many so-called serious television programmes on commercial channels.

Meeting Urban Change

Traditionally, marketing directors prided themselves on developing a strategy and an implementation that would reach their 'publics'. Effective programmes were defined as those which had a structure the marketing teams considered efficient, enabling them to use the most appropriate media to deliver the message to that public cohort. It was accepted that if the message could be delivered through a number of different channels, such as hard copy magazines, television, radio, and perhaps arts or sports sponsorship, it was more likely to be noted and understood, and more importantly remembered, than if all the eggs were thrown into one basket, such as newspaper or television advertising.

As business leaders move forward in their thinking and hopefully have noted our earlier chapters, they will fundamentally refine their communication processes. The right delivery systems in terms of media choice will generate tighter definitions of target cohorts they hope to reach. Crossing research data between the message cohort and the readership or viewing audience will, when integrated, sharpen the effectiveness of the programme. The effectiveness of primary communications becomes dramatically apparent. The marketing function should interact in the future much more closely with individual Board members who should understand the product development and the overriding corporate identity. They will be more capable of drawing these strings together if they embrace some of the academic disciplines like semiotics and the neuro-psychology of decision making as part of their business training. Such cross-fertilisation can jointly shape societal mores. This will become more apparent in the future as online research provides layer upon layer of information on who their target audience is and when they absorb socio-cultural ideas. Managers will do this through the application of adjacent academic disciplines such as critical discourse analysis (CDA) managers. Through such techniques they will have before them cohort members' histories like never before. The data they extract will offer the 'how, why and where' to explain why their target publics hold the attitudes they do. An understanding of community attitudes and what influences those attitudes means managers will better understand the global opinions that influence the international media that is shaping the views of their own national, regional and local journalists who write copy that may not necessarily be in the interests of boardroom strategists.

The Economist's 'World in 2014' publication has a Business section titled 'After the Famine', written by the indefatigable *Financial Times* columnist Lucy Kellaway (*The Economist*, 2013c) in which she suggests that, despite there being steady forecasts for an economic upturn in the coming years:

That doesn't mean that working life in 2014 is going to be comfortable – or uncompetitive. Who is up and who is down will be decided less by Machiavellian scheming than by data. Companies will start assessing people according to how well they do on social networks. Nobody will be interested in simple statistics such as numbers of followers or moronic clicking on 'like' buttons.

Instead, a host of sophisticated algorithmic tools will increasingly be taken seriously. Everyone will learn to understand new maps that plot the extent of their social influence. The article, goes on to say:

The years ahead will witness another large stride towards the paperless office. The under 30s who never understood the point of paper anyway, will convert the straggler. Anyone who insists on turning up to meetings with hard copy will look laughably yesterday. As everyone turns to tablets and the devices go on getting smaller, communications will become briefer. Jargon will still be manager's language of choice but each helping of it will be smaller. Bullet points can expect a corker of a year ahead.

The view expressed earlier that the street and restaurant as office has now disappeared is reinforced by Kellaway when she finishes her article by saying:

Companies are starting to fret that years of virtual working emailing the person working in the next cubicle have created workforces that don't know each other. The remedy will be mandatory social integration days in which everyone will be compelled to show up at work and is randomly assigned half a dozen colleagues to have lunch with. It will be pretty painful and unpopular.

No doubt the concept as she sees it will, if extended, bring back the street and town market place as office!

Summary

1.   Previous chapters (1, 2 and 3) have discussed the abstract social and governmental pressures on business and organisational change. This chapter has shifted the emphasis towards a wave of change through urbanisation that will increasingly impact every one of the societal changes we forecast.

2.   Global urbanisation is proceeding at a significant rate, yet is hardly noticed in the short term by individuals, especially those who will feel its impact on their business, cultural and political lives. In 2050 half the world's population will live in towns and cities. This provides an effective vehicle to help national and international organisations generate powerful stakeholder interaction.

3.   As these pressures gather pace, future leaders must understand the process of government in greater depth and realise how decisions at even local, as well as national and international levels, are made.

4.   The processes of urbanisation and the impact of academic and cultural life on that process must be understood by, at a truly workers level, world leaders. It is not enough to rely on media reporting alone.

Chapter 5
New Missions for Old Cultures

In Chapter 4 we emphasised the rather obvious but frequently ignored factor that societal changes are a response to leadership attitudes. Urbanisation is not an abstract force, a gravitational pressure driven by unconscious forces. People decide to move into towns and such contextual changes generate new leaders who themselves influence each other. How those changes generate new cultures, which establish fresh accepted beliefs and values, depends on a cascade of leadership hierarchies. In knowledge-based societies where the understanding of decisions is identified by the media, the acceptance of all decisions by a wider public varies according to the professional application of communication techniques. Leaders must accept their responsibility to explain and accept they live in a collaborative society. Having spent many decades advising corporate leaders within global companies, it has already surprised us how frequently senior managers believe their decisions relate solely to the problem at hand. Every decision influences other decisions or indeed other intellectual thought processes among management groups with which they work. Later in this chapter we summarise this psychological phenomenon with a sub-heading referring to the process of 'collaborative ties that bind, a network of shared values' which underpins many of the arguments described throughout this book.

The factors discussed in the previous chapter are all significant and chief executives would be wise to consider as part of what is frequently called 'managerial reinvention' which is a 'reinvention' of old cultures. Traditionally many appointments of CEOs followed the route of internal promotion based on internal preference. This could often be guided by debate as to who would cause the least problem if rejected. Today, and increasingly so in the future, the appointment is a response to shareholder pressure. This can be by way of the chairman or in periods of mergers and acquisitions, a choice moulded from agreement between buyer and seller. The company taking over will not always determine who will head the new operation. Headhunters, as consultants, may have an over-arching role, if only to provide alternatives. Whoever provides the traction it is unlikely in the current climate to be a response to the type of pressures described. Time pressure can force a quick decision, yet this is the moment when the choice should be of someone who has the intellectual skills to develop a new mission for the company. A mission that will ensure organisations respond to future societal changes adumbrated in Chapter 4 as a response to urbanisation.

Reorienting Capital

Possibly the most important societal changes will be an acceptance of capitalism in a new form where business organisations play a more prominent role in community life. William (Bill) George, Professor of Management at Harvard Business School, writing in management consultant McKinsey's *Insights* publication, says he does not 'subscribe to the notion that companies exist to create value for shareholders. I think they are there to create value for the customers. I think we have to reorient how we think about capitalism, which is going through a major transformation. We need global leadership'. Later in the article he states: 'Do not let your shareholders manage you. You have to manage them. You have to say what you are going to do or to be, here's our strategy, here's the team we're putting in place, and here are the tactics. And then you have to buy time to get it done.' In the final section of the article under the heading 'Where Boards Go Wrong' he maintains that the:

> ... board's job is to stabilise. The board's number one goal is to ensure that the company has the right mission and values and that it follows that, it has the right leadership that will reinforce that and the succession coming along behind it and that it has the strategic goals for the company that provide them winning strategies globally. Any company that doesn't create better value for its customers than its competitors do will be out of business. So if you start with just meeting shareholder's needs, you may be out of business in ten years.

Change with the Facts

Before discussing a fresh approach to the stakeholder function it is important to understand and perhaps accept key changes taking place since the economic downturn, regarding what the *Financial Times* refers to as 'New Facts of Finance' (2013f) in an article by Gillian Tett. She opens the piece with a quotation from an anonymous English economist who she says remarked, 'When the facts change, I change my mind.' This is an important statement and underpins the financial changes taking place, which underpin the cultural changes underlying this chapter's title. Tett's feature lists eight financial changes a senior banker reflected to her. In summary they can be listed here as:

1.   Bigger is no longer presumed to mean better. Investors once (before 2008) cooed with admiration when they saw gigantic banks. No longer. We know that economies of scale are sometimes an illusion.

2.   Finance is no longer viewed as self-financing. On the contrary it often seems self-destructing.

3.   We know taxpayers are on the hook when finance goes wrong; no one vaguely hopes that a magic wand will wave problems away.

4.   Leverage matters.

5.   Liquidity matters too. Before 2008 financial innovation seemed to have liquefied most asset classes. Today everyone knows liquidity can vanish, usually when most needed.

6.   Bubbles do not exist in baths. Policy makers liked to think they could mop up after excesses rather than intervene in advance. No longer.

7.   Structural solutions are not taboo. Before 2008 it was almost outlandish to suggest policy makers might deliberately shape the direction of finance with policy interventions.

8.   Previously, the non-financial sector was generally ignored. Today policy makers and investors alike want to shine a spotlight on shadow banks and governments belatedly want to create some controls.

She goes on to say that 'one of the biggest and most important cultural shifts concerns the role of government'. The crucial issue is that assumptions can stealthily change, in ways we barely notice. Which is why we need to ponder our ideas and then ask ourselves another question: could this conventional wisdom shift again in the next five years?

Tett's article in the *Financial Times* identifies important financial developments that relate to the underlying cultural changes we are discussing throughout this book.

The Stakeholder Function

References to stakeholder functions should mean more than a communications programme of sending newsletters and copying press releases to interested government officers, financial analysts and hub company suppliers. Taking the last group as an example, the positive action would be for the hub company to work with their suppliers to help increase their profitability and turnover. This can be achieved by secondment of an executive to advise the supplier as an external consultant. If the supplier can be helped to become more profitable then they will be expected and helped to develop new products, new services and possibly provide a more efficient service to the stakeholder's buyers. If that process, which truly involves the supplier's stakeholders, is extended into enough large institutions and companies, it will achieve micro changes, which could and should evolve into a new face for the capitalist concept.

Leadership and Company Culture

Leadership still requires hard skills to generate bottom-line success but it has to be underpinned by an emotional reaction that responds to external social change and in turn influences positively the organisations' own culture. This response to the wider community will be to the advantage of the hub organisation as well as its stakeholders. The CEO will need to consider the involvement of new types of non-executive director who will become closely involved in the organisations culture and bring in an extra dimension in terms of skills and attitudes. In Chapter 7 we discuss the potential for inclusion of what may appear to be irrelevant academic subjects ranging through neuropsychology, CDA, semiotics and of course communications theory itself. Carefully selected non-executive directors can be a source of new thinking, which can be injected into boardroom strategy.

No one person, however brilliant, can carry the whole gamut of new skills that will become increasingly valuable in the future, even if they strengthen leadership success, but non-executive directors can, if chosen with care, reflect the culture needs and vision for the company and ensure the chief executive's vision is underpinned by values. The result will be less concern by directors with social networking and reinforcing boardroom decisions but more interest in helping the company achieve success within its global community. Interaction with the external community, whether it is business or otherwise, is significantly important but so is internal intra-departmental relations, which must be seen as of equal value. This is an area where non-executive director appointments can play an influential role. The essential element in the process is to see these concepts where the organisation, and the community within which it operates, have an underlying purpose. As one business colleague said informally to the authors, 'Business schools need to provide more than tools to achieve bottom-line results but to maximise returns in terms of a balance between stakeholder interests and the concerns of the company itself.'

The Economist's Schumpeter columnist (*The Economist*, 2013e) takes a cynical view of boardroom culture which would no doubt include the selection process that

> *… boards have been largely ceremonial institutions: friends of the boss who meet every few months to rubber-stamp his decisions and have a good lunch. Critics have compared directors to 'parsley on fish', decorative but ineffectual; or honorary colonels, 'ornamental in parade but fairly useless in battle'. Ralph Nader called them 'cuckolds' who are always the last to know when managers have erred. The corporate scandals of the early 2000s forced boards to take a more active role. … This led to a big increase in the quality of boards.*

The *Economist* article (2013e) goes on to discuss the book *Boards that Lead* by Ram Charan, Dennis Carey and Michael Useen (2013) which says that Boards are in the midst of a third revolution, they are becoming strategic partners. They base their arguments on detailed knowledge of the world's boardroom. Later Schumpeter (*The Economist*, 2013e) queries: 'How can you make sure boards can add value rather than subtract it? And how do you make sure that boards that lead do not create warring centres of power? The first is that boards should focus on providing companies with strategic advice. Boardrooms contain too many people with different priorities: corporate veterans who give lectures on how they would have handled things; egomaniacs who like to show how much they know about everything; hobby horse jockeys who mount the same steed regardless of the race; captives of compliance who are obsessed with box ticking.'

Despite these criticisms Schumpeter takes a positive position later in the review of the book, reflecting that Boards are getting better at dealing with these problems and suggests they are getting better at recruiting high flyers and 'ditching ground scrapers'. Boards should focus on getting their relationships with the CEO right. 'It is not enough to act as monitors,' it says, they need to act as personal mentors and high-level talent scouts. Their final paragraph concludes: 'Are organisations that meet a dozen times a year capable of offering strategic advice in a fast paced world?'

The Multitasking Leader

The above issues need to be considered within the context of leadership training. Core business training and the need to widen boundaries of knowledge by driving ownership stakes into nearby fields will intensify in coming years. The chief executive's prior training at a strategic geopolitical level will have to become increasingly broad-minded, in business terms. As my co-author (RH) once remarked in a lecture on corporate decision making:

> It is not a case of relating decision making only to the geographical areas where it is marketing products or where its headquarters office is situated. Stakeholder geography no longer selects the data required. All trade is now international, if not at primary level, then at secondary levels where its own stakeholders are being influenced.

Chief executives in the decades ahead will have to behave like sponges and absorb knowledge and new skills from areas that may not be recognised as relevant or understood in their complexity. Chapter 6 discusses in detail selected elements of adjacent disciplines in the belief that a reader who is aiming to achieve high office might study methodologies frequently used in non-managerial disciplines and learn from the application of such new processes.

Research carried out by The UK Marketing Society in 2013 consisted of asking 50 successful chief executives what were the essential skills needed for success as a leader. Many of the answers were what would be expected, but the important element was that all these factors were important and all should be taken on board in terms of business training. The eight essentials were said to be:

1.   give a clear sense of direction;

2.   bring the customer into the boardroom;

3.   communicate clearly inside and out;

4.   be flexible but not sloppy;

5.   take risks but don't bet the company;

6.   build the team around you;

7.   listen with humility, act with courage;

8.   earn your reward through building trust.

Bearing in mind the new but intense pressures likely to develop in coming years, we would add one more necessary skill. That is for chief executives to be capable of underpinning strategy through their own knowledge of every function, to be capable of talking the talk with department heads. This does not mean the chief executive should be capable of doing the jobs of others but they should know enough to carry out informed discussion and jointly with their specialist managers make decisions that they fully understand. We have commented earlier on our surprise at the ignorance of many senior managers as to how government, for example, actually works and the process by which geopolitical decisions are made, nationally, internationally and even within their own local community authorities.

The Media Function

The same can be said about the all-important communications function. Certainly no chief executive should be exposed to a media interrogation without pre-briefing and rehearsal but when it comes to the development of a full reputation-building programme leaders must now be capable of discussion of the detail in an informed manner and not just as a listener. The same applies to human resource strategy, finance and investment, not to forget of course product marketing. Most chief executives have a skill in one of these areas but in coming years that will not be enough. Only a strategic-level knowledge in the tool-kit will be enough to survive the competition. Many business degrees, even at MBA level, attempt to involve their students in such disciplines but any reality check will identify shortages of lecturers in these areas. Some business schools overcome the problem by building their own relationships with external consultants or academics established in these specialisms. But solutions are not easy to find. There is a need, indeed a demand, for freelance lecturers who can talk the talk of chief executive requirements while coaching specialist's skills drawn from their practical application at grassroots level. Every one of the specialist disciplines mentioned are available within their respective professional bodies for freelance coaching. The failure of so many business schools and colleges to draw on such experience is a lacuna that needs filling urgently.

Ann Francke, Chief Executive of the UK's Chartered Management Institute (CMI), argues that managerial reinvention applies to the need to reward senior executives for improving the bottom line rather than just cutting costs and jobs. She suggests that business schools should focus more on skills that matter – such as communication, performance management, change management and teamwork – rather than sticking rigidly to outdated core syllabuses that have not been regularly renewed and redefined. We with leadership training and the need to reinvent the MBA in Chapter 6.

Francke proposes that professional bodies – such as those for Law, Accounting, Marketing, Public Relations, Human Resource Management and others – should put greater emphasis on management practice. She describes how the CMI are launching all-party parliamentary inquiries on management and leadership to seek an end to management practices that undermine growth.

Only managers who raise the bar of their theoretical knowledge and professional skills will survive due to increasingly professional competition. We argue that internal business models must not only encapsulate the plethora of internal and external factors discussed but they should evolve as a primary response mechanism to change.

The Corporate Business Plan

The Corporate Business Plan (CBP) can frequently be analysed as a structural matrix for debate on a company's strategy because the process of their preparation is multifunctional and usually involves an internal range of senior managers. Its preparation can involve cultural and attitudinal debate at every stage. Its preparation, even if the final draft is to acquire status regarding the Chairman or CEO's vision for the company ahead of the completion of that year's business plan, is still restricted to that financial year. We can use the business plan as a discussion vehicle to encapsulate many elements considered throughout this book. This choice of the CBP is for convenience and not because CBPs are the best design in content terms to act as crystal balls describing the CEO's future hopes and aspirations. They have one essential weakness. Their emphasis is frequently on short-term factors like bottom-line profits, the dangers of upcoming government policy and how the company should respond to that policy, an assessment of current management strengths (and weaknesses) that may require a restructuring of functional management along with corporate and product marketing strategy. Depending on the quality of internal security and perhaps merger and acquisition (M&A) intentions, the plan will still be considered within that financial year rather than looking further forward.

This over-emphasis on the short term was the theme of a May 2013 conference address in Canada entitled 'Focusing on the Long Term', by Dominic Barton, Global Managing Director of McKinsey, to the Institute of Corporate Directors. His hypothesis in the speech boiled down to three words:

Patience

Promotes

Prosperity

He argued that too much emphasis on the short term damages corporate values and there was significant potential value created by refocusing businesses on the longer term. His closing summary statement suggested there were six factors involved in avoiding short-term thinking and emphasised the longer term for effective business planning.

His six factors are:

1.   asset owner-led collaboration;

2.   engagement platforms;

3.   activated passive holdings;

4.   agreed engagement principles for the institutional investor;

5.   for the Boards of Directors there should be long-term value committees;

6.   comprehension models that reflect the views of workload directors, with rewards for them over a product of risk cycles with a process of integrated reporting rather than quarterly earnings.

The answers, he said, were in the hands of those in the audience, that is, corporate directors.

This author (Watts) still remembers the view expressed to him by the chief executive of one of the UK's largest consultancy firms that he knew what recommendations needed to go into client business plans within a few days after appointment but had to carry out three to four months of research and interviews to justify the fees and convince the CEO of the consultant's personal judgement. At that time, despite the evolution of corporate management structures from the immediate post-war military style, and later using methodologies that emanated from US and UK business schools, there resulted an over-rigid consistency for CBP content that embraced an almost cliché list of headings. This list included:

- product assessments including New Product Development (NPD);

- forecasts of changes to their industry during the 12 months ahead;

- target audience generalisations;

- competition profiles, their corporate and product positioning;

- customer attitudes to their products;

- the state of the company's existing management; and finally

- a detailed programme of action, all with budgets.

It is generally accepted that the growth of the management consultancy profession in the UK grew from the demand by British senior managers in the 1950s and 60s for training in the application of the new management theories that appeared at that time in academic papers by business school researchers. The management structures suggested then have changed little since the 1960s, regardless of the more recent improvements that have been made.

Reaching the Public Audience

Despite new ingredients and metrics in most business plans there have only been small variations in many function headings and such headings over time have passed into the realm of history in terms of their usefulness. Their relevance to environmental change and the new pressures forecast earlier make many function headings obsolete. In planning terms so much social data is obsolete by the time it is presented to senior management. Time is the damaging force of correction.

In the political, business and economic environment it is not updated metrics but the dramatic breakdown of the total lexicon that may become the manager's poison chalice in decades ahead. An example is exemplified when marketing and communications departments plan their programmes and the message delivery systems they intend to use. In doing this as usual they will attempt to identify and record the lifestyles of corporate and product audiences. In classic marketing textbook style they will attempt to assemble what they consider and hope to be accurate lifestyle definitions for their publics. Perhaps they will attempt that for all or part of important cohorts within the 18 to 49 age group. We select this age range as a significant group for any organisation or manufacturer because they control massive spending power – $990 billion annually in the US alone and probably influence another $400 billion globally. Such a group is not an insignificant audience regardless of product or functional sales operations. In fact in its totality it is a significant proportion of the world's population in terms of lifestyle generally. It is thus important as a community for any marketing message or reputation projection to reach. Their role as receivers of products, information or concepts is immensely significant.

As a group, Millenials are discussed in some detail by journalist Emily Steel in a *Financial Times* article (2013a) entitled 'Generation Next'. She bases her comments on current psycho-qualitative and quantitative research and states that this generation is the first adult population who have no known life without instant messaging or access to the web. They live in an 'on-demand media' world and do not feel the need to own any part of it. They pay little attention to big broadcasters or traditional culture tastemakers but assimilate hot trends via social media, 'under the radar of adults older than 30'.

The group she discusses is half the 18–49 age group of the world's population. Research results suggest that the respondents do not care about being rich or being good looking. In fact they cynically see through any marketing or promotional programme. They are optimistic, civic minded and self-expressive. By the next decade (2020–24), this age group, the Millennials, will constitute half the world's population of 18–49 year olds. They are spending less time watching TV, more time watching video (which is more on demand via digital) and, instead of channel surfing, they spend time with 'venture content' which gives them a role in creating the programming they prefer, which are edgy short programmes. According to Emily Steel this is a generation that has popularised the sharing economy, where they are more comfortable renting dresses or a car than owning them. Social currency comes with being in the know and sharing that knowledge on Twitter, Facebook and Instagram.

CBPs and their functional analytical headings, if considered individually within the context of defining a corporation's public for corporate messaging and not just for the marketing of products and concepts, presents new problems. In the coming decade, as managers prepare their CBPs, they will attempt to define, isolate and understand a third of the global population for a multiplicity of reasons, but they will find this group does not read or identify with standard media delivery systems, rejects marketing and sales messages as essentially untruthful and prefers to be integrated personally into the creative process. When the Millennials were first identified as a target group, occupying such a large portion of the world's high-spending decision makers, the response by marketing professionals was to dismiss them as a group that would disappear and return to the audience norm as age took its hold. However, research has shown this not to be the case. Habits acquired in the early stages of life influenced, sometimes partially and sometime totally, by the lifestyle norms described above, are likely to continue past the age of 40, possibly for longer.

The above is only one area that when investigated identifies changes new CEOs must absorb into their personal skill set. It is not enough to pass all responsibility to the marketing department, the changes are too wide ranging and they need be considered within a wider strategy. Such changes in the structure of the business plan constitute only one part of the total. Changes will continue as decision makers among corporate stakeholders demand increasingly accurate data on which to base decisions. The previous paragraph identified only one area of change within one population group. This is not the only area where the business manager, whether an MBA graduate or a learn-by-experience advocates, must re-manage skills and acquire new methodologies. This is despite the frequent comments in the media that it is more important to learn on the job than to acquire academic qualifications. The opposite is the truth and will become more so in the decade ahead.

In the creative service industries it is accepted that the 'sitting next to Nelly' approach to training engenders later a brand of middle managers who know and understand only the one aspect of their function because they have not received the theoretical underpinning that provides the tools to attack new problems and develop wider solutions.

Enlarging the Tool Box

It is not our purpose in this chapter to discuss the changing needs of the MBA syllabus (we do that in Chapter 7) nor is it to provide 'how to' solutions, but we do argue for a wider academic understanding of new skills that hitherto played little or no role in day-to-day management practice.

In the coming decade many pressures will fall on leaders of organisations whether they are managing small to medium-sized enterprises (SMEs) or heading up massive transnationals. New strictures will still be there and they will continue to change in response to global political and cultural evolution. Such changes have already been suggested and we have identified their importance not only in terms of the bottom line and the intensity of competitor pressures but also because political and social pressures will intensify. It will not be effective to continue in the same old ways and hope the training of earlier years will see senior managers through. The managers of the decade ahead must become lifelong students. The success-oriented corporations, not to mention NGOs and geopolitical bodies, will expect senior staff to continue the learning process past the initial learning phase of their younger lives. There are many adjacent disciplines applicable to management and these will almost certainly be embraced increasingly by managers wanting to sharpen their management skills and who realise there are academic disciplines ready to absorb.

It is not easy to identify these areas. They are not often seen wearing new clothes. For example, social and visual semiotics is a quasi-psychological area normally listed within the philosophy faculty at universities. Currently it is being recognised by creative service professionals as important for business use also. The majority of business leaders are honing their traditional skills, yet they frequently fail to appreciate that visual media has become dominant in terms of transposing ideas and concepts as more easily understood by target audiences.

The decades ahead will demand an understanding of disciplines that 'talk' in visual terms. Such disciplines are usually seen as of academic relevance, only they are not. The business environment will intensify competitively and it will be those who embrace the skills that were once seen as applicable only to academia but are now understood to have business relevance too. Semiotic theory considered as a literary and philosophical discipline is one example.

Another is narrative theory which is usually applied to literary criticism. It is valuable to consider these disciplines in detail, not only as a teaching process that will help future managers, which it will, but because they provide examples of how the process of reaching out to 'foreign' concepts and applying them to management could identify one route they should take if they intend to compete managerially and stride forward. The two disciplines interact in places, but later in Chapter 7 we discuss the use of relevant academic disciplines in more detail. This should hopefully explain why managers need to understand and apply such fresh disciplines that will strengthen their competitive skills. In an age of the visual, social semiotics is being seen as one discipline integral to effective communication in management. Strangely it is being found that senior managers have difficulty expressing their message in visual terms. Communications managers, usually with a background in the written word, are comfortable with their written material. Unfortunately most of them are visually illiterate.

Earlier we discussed the cascade effect of chief executives and indeed the chairman's influence throughout an organisation's culture, depending who is the most respected within a company. Respect derives less from repetitive statements concerning corporate culture but more from the translation of that culture into lifestyles, decision making by senior staff and how those decisions relate to the daily life of an organisation. Top managers' attitudes and personal vision must relate to its practical application of the corporate culture and its obviously apparent internalisation within the behaviour of that chief executive or chairman regarding small as well as the big decisions.

The successful middle, as well as senior, manager should be adept at contextual intra-disciplines. It is not enough to rely on corporate strengths in separate disciplines such as financial management, product development or indeed talented staff alone. The ability to understand and generate interaction between disciplines is needed within a more technical understanding of the context within which each operates.

As one chief executive recently commented: 'Managers can no longer remain in a garden of remembrance as if time has stood still since they qualified.' Business school graduates preparing for leadership in the decade ahead will find a need to broaden their training constituency and avoid the straightjacket of earlier training. External consultants can usually identify the age of managers by the business school jargon and theories they employ. It is not enough to broaden the range of traditional disciplines that inform the old decision making. There must be a well-researched understanding of the impact of one discipline upon another within their respective contexts. For example, a manager has to understand the application and development of social media on off-line communication, No function within a company can be reliant on the effectiveness of its internal and external communications across each stakeholder without maintaining regular monitoring through research. It is remarkable that when we carry out internal monitoring research how many staff had not read internal newsletters in hard copy or online, or worse read them while thinking of something else so cannot answer the simplest questions on content.

A company's specialist departments are obviously important in the development of its wider IT strategy, ditto with external public affairs, reputation management and indeed financial policy. However senior managers' personal training should include sufficient technical knowledge of most managerial disciplines to understand the full impact of any development within function areas. Even the most specialist discipline, and indeed managerial organisations, is international and has therefore to maintain a wider systemic monitoring process that tracks global cultural change and how it is interacting within the inherent region.

Exploiting online media may well sharpen the external profile or image but management now has to maintain high levels of technical knowledge within each discipline as an ingredient that provides traction for corporate strategy. This means senior managers can only define strategy if they understand public policy decisions and the international cultures within their markets and those which influence the total market. Business graduates at MBA level will have to understand the reason for most financial legislation changes internationally. They will need to track new research in social science, genetics, robotics and even nanotechnology. All such elements will, in the next few years, change society beyond recognition. The skill is to understand the implications of change and when to draw in specialist suppliers to explain the detail. Reliance on the media is not enough.

Business school degree syllabuses at Master's level will increasingly need to offer longer courses so there is time to train students to separate social change from current fads. They will need to know that they as individuals have to serve as corporate monitors, checking public policy and the pressures that arise from the media, from governments and sometimes demographic change. Increasingly it is the CEO's role to understand how and why change takes place and whether it meets public expectations. As stated earlier, the CEO lives in a network of shared values, or should do!

Perception and reputation management are not enough on their own. They are only delivery systems for an already agreed strategy. Lacunae between corporate objectives and how such objectives are to be met within stakeholder cohorts will only be filled if senior managers understand the technical disciplines which affect their decision making. To borrow from a recent political conference in the UK, modern business training must be about 'The One Company'. It is not a loosely bound packet of functions. Effectiveness is lost if the impact on each other and their changing contexts is not recognised early.

In essence a business degree should teach managers who are aiming for leadership that they should analyse for themselves 'what is the problem and how can it be solved, and avoid the belief that product marketing is separate from corporate reputation as if each is a specialised discipline'. Product support along with market research relates back to company reputation even when that reputation is filtered through intermediate stages at subsidiary and strategic business unit (SBU) level.

Product communications may in the long run be part of corporate reputation but even at that level corporate communications can derive and change under the influence of international pressures of different ideas. Both are intertwined and the future for a corporation is to ensure managers at every level are trained in a range of disciplines that include internal and external communications skills which embrace areas such as CSR and its impact on reputation management. As we argue in Chapter 6, the corporate MBA will, in the coming decade, increasingly aim to attract students with wide backgrounds and qualifications – students who will know they must become sensors of the social trends that not only help formulate policy but enable organisations to adapt and understand communications. The discipline of corporate affairs is no longer a container for internal and external message delivery but an integral part of the decision-making process. Change will occur faster than ever. This means that managers at all levels have to be involved in each step from analysis to action,

If we see the intensity of environmental and cultural change at the level discussed earlier, new pressures will be placed on MBA syllabuses to respond to those changes described in some detail later. They discuss, among other things, the transcription of hitherto academic disciplines to management practice. This author (RW), as an external university examiner, has frequently argued at faculty meetings the importance of adding newly developing fields to the Master's degree curriculum. The response has consistently been the same: 'No time. There are many such areas we would like to add but this could add a full year to the degree.' Bearing in mind the range of different pressures that will fall on leaders in the coming years it is obvious that the solution is not to include them under specialist MBAs. Nor is the solution to fit them all in at a superficial level. The danger of being a 'Jack of all trades', a descriptor too easily applied, will not prepare a potential leader to make an adequate response to so many changing pressures.

It may be that the MBA will need to be linked to specialist degrees making use of the newly evolving part-time Massive Open Online Courses (MOOCs). Leading universities are increasingly offering MOOCs. They are free in the sense that students can watch, learn and train through the lectures, which are generally of a high standard (but not always!). Some of the courses have over a quarter of a million students globally. The costs are carried by the universities through extra personal interaction with tutors, payment for accreditation certificates and of course through sales of supporting textbooks. They are only in their early stages but with enormous potential to combine on an 'as and when' basis with full-time work they will help chief executives in the creation of large cohorts of different levels of management and achieve a wider range of skills than could be reached through in-house training on its own.

There is no easy answer to the build-up of pressures we forecast and certainly a response will be expected from any CEOs taking a new appointment. The MOOC movement is revolutionising higher education because they bring training and education to a massive audience that perhaps cannot reach a university or college. However the fallout rate is high as would be expected, but for the universities it draws new student into awareness of their brand. They will offer immediate responses to company needs and have a flexibility that will show raised standards of business knowledge across staff management at all levels. Nothing is certain, but the revolution is happening and will intensify. In the next chapter we continue the dialogue on the application of academic areas to the changing needs of corporate management.

Summary

1. Leaders must be sufficiently multi-skilled to maintain informed discourse with *all* function heads, especially during the development of longer-term strategy and business plans.

2. The business strategy in future must prioritise relationships with every stakeholder, often to their advantage, helping through secondment of mangers to improve stakeholder management skills.

3.   Training opportunities should be exploited through MOOCs and other systems to raise standards. Non-executive directors can provide a reservoir of new disciplines to Boards and also improve departmental relations at operational levels.

4.   The global challenges we envisage can only be met through leadership at a level which involves collaborative paradigms and which ties together a network of shared values.

Chapter 6

Their Story is Now Your Story

This chapter is concerned with the importance of shifting the emphasis of corporate strategy and communications from what the company wants to say, to messages that reflect the interests and mores of external publics with their wider outlook and changing attitudes. Shaping corporate reputation to fit societal changes will be less about 'we want' and more about reflecting what the global public wants.

There has been a logical sequence in the development of our argument throughout this book. Earlier chapters were concerned with current attitudes and in some areas the continuation of the past in terms of what we might term staged progress. As consultants with experience in the analysis of management attitudes and culture we observed through our primary research, or indeed our initial discussions at the first point of client contact, an enormous range of different attitudes, knowledge levels and indeed business skills.

In the majority of cases, regardless of nationality and the organisation's size or indeed the industry sector involved, there was an obvious need for external analysis. This is frequently realised by the client often at the most senior level. Sometimes the realisation follows a merger of two organisations between what was initially believed by both sides to be complementary cultures. Both Boards of Directors in the excitements of the merger frequently consider, usually erroneously, that 'both Boards of Directors have similar views on the way forward'. This was frequently found to be far from the reality too late to make adjustments to the legal contracts. That knowledge, often of an abstract nature, may well have changed the timing and content of the merger agreement if differences had been identified and described in terms of their application at an early stage of the due diligence analysis which sadly concentrates almost entirely on the financial elements.

Frequently, a new chief executive is appointed who was considered by senior managers as someone who would be more responsive to change if the blame could be hoisted onto an external consultant's shoulders! For SMEs the starting point is frequently more obvious: turnover and bottom-line figures had been stationary for too long and pressures were building from within the organisation that 'we are not responding to new markets and beating the competition'.

Whatever the original desire for advice or the need for change, what was remarkable was the range of management skills to be found at every level.

Chapter by chapter we have identified the remarkable range of intellectual threads listed in our visual diagram. This forms a summary at the start of the book. We termed it 'meeting the global challenge' and listed what we have called a collaborative paradigm of the many pressures developing like seeds in a half-tended garden which, if untended, can take over the wider landscape.

In Chapters 4 and 5 we expanded the narrative with particular emphasis on societal and environmental changes that are driving the pressures on every organisation, whether it is governmental, NGO, business or the arts. All such changes are led by leaders who are thankfully responding to the increasingly sophisticated cultures of business school teaching and allied internal training systems. These collaborative threads should eventually bundle into unstoppable rivers of thought that can only meet the future global challenges we discuss by means of the visible corporate reputation. The methodologies we suggest describe the 'how to' process that must underpin this fundamental change of direction from 'this is us, the organisation speaking' to 'this is now your story reflected in our story which reflects yours'.

The words corporate reputation, corporate image, corporate communications, corporate identity and company positioning have related meanings. Senior managers will offer a variety of their own definitions. For example, corporate image is an omnibus term used by the public and business world to describe in adjectival terms what comes to mind when a specific company name is projected. Professional communications consultants tend to avoid the word 'image' because of the laxity of its definition.

The phrase corporate identity would be the most accurate descriptor for much of the work discussed in this book but unfortunately the design and graphics profession have taken possession of the phrase to describe logo design, typography and the overall visual presentation of a company and its attributes. This function has attracted increasingly well-qualified practitioners in the last few decades. As a result, corporate identity as a phrase should be avoided in the context of this chapter, which is concerned with corporate reputation. This is despite the fact that design companies feel qualified to discuss their client's corporate strategy on the grounds that the visual presentation of any organisation 'speaks' on behalf of its underlying strategy. In fact we argue that corporate design is more correctly a representation of the underlying corporate policy and strategy.

The visual elements involved in opinion formation and attitude change were discussed in Chapter 6 within a more detailed context, but they are significant in psychological terms. The German Nazi Party in the 1930s made wide use of such flagrant symbolism. This should not detract from its importance to any manager's understanding of visual language and what it means in the context of corporate reputation. In Chapter 6 we discussed methodologies which could embrace the discipline of visual semiotics as an example of how some academic areas can be considered as integral to business communications and corporate identity.

It is important to understand and identify the interaction of many corporate reputation disciplines that unconsciously come to embrace wider philosophical beliefs of morality, ethics and academic validity which are frequently carried along on the luggage rack of the communications carriage of corporate message delivery systems. The validity or otherwise of this broad field in its totality, when seen within the context of company reputation, tends to be assembled as if it all added up to a single meaning. The leaders of major global institutions will increasingly need to dissect and identify every element in this complex business directory.

This has become apparent when bodies such as the UK Financial Conduct Authority (FCA) complain publicly that industry places profits over ethics and that workers must take responsibility for their actions rather than waiting for regulators to step in. As an example the Director of the FCA, Tracy McDermott (FCA, 2013), considers 'the financial services industry is just a microcosm of wider society ... that is why firms must grasp the nettle and actually embed cultural values that champion positive behaviour and make clear that there is no room for misconduct. Only then will we arrive at a place where people do not regard the behaviour we have seen as acceptable'.

We discuss in this chapter the process by which a corporation, or any organisation for that matter, should develop its own identity in such a way that no external communicator can accuse it of adopting obvious attributes like motherhood and honesty rather than more complex and difficult achievements such as loyalty, trust and social acceptance. It is the methodology a company can apply to establish a clear positioning for itself in its global environment.

Our aim is to help in that establishment of a positioning that will project in a certain way an organisation's name and its relationship to its products, services and management philosophy. There is a concept known as 'monolithic branding', where the product brand name is the same as the manufacturer's name. An obvious example is Coca-Cola, Ford or Gillette. In such cases the positioning analysis and methodology aims for a comprehensive set of descriptors which are clearly part of the marketing process with the logical and creative parameters this demands.

We are concerned here, however, with positioning as a statement that will represent any organisation in it totality and reflects corporate culture, corporate philosophy and relationships with stakeholders. Establishing such a positioning is more than simply creating an advertising campaign which artificially papers over the corporation's beliefs with slogans and attractive visuals. Such areas are normally dreamt up by creative communications bodies such as advertising, public relations, direct marketing and online consultants employing social media.

Establishing a Corporate Persona

The process of establishing an organisation's positioning is complex and includes a range of ethical, moral and strategic management philosophies that sometimes dictate boardroom decisions for many years ahead. It is not a superficial process developed by the directors at weekend task force meetings in a comfortable conference centre somewhere in the countryside. In many ways the Board of Directors are the least competent to establish long-term positioning statements about a company. Such internal discussions at boardroom level tend to support the triumph of hope over reality. In our experience interviews we have carried out with individual directors generate a wide range of responses when senior managers are asked to describe their company at a social function. Usually such questions generate eight different views from every six directors. Some replies differ in substance or emphasis in response to the same question even when put to the chairperson or CEO.

This does not mean there are fundamental differences of policy but that positioning strategy is seldom a regular item on Board agendas. Decisions requiring immediate action occupy a large part of most Board meeting discussions in our experience which means wide-ranging discussion on the company's strategy and positioning within different market and regions get marginalised.

Views about positioning may not differ in fundamental terms but more likely they will differ in emphasis. Interviews carried out with members of the Board of a large automobile manufacturer by this author (RW) as part of a communications positioning analysis asked: 'How would you respond at a social event to the question what do you do?' The replies include a number of different answers such as: 'I work for one of Europe's leading car manufacturers'; ' I work for a large Birmingham manufacturer'; 'I work in the car industry'; 'I'm with one of the big Northern metal bashers'(!); 'I work for a motor parts manufacturer'; 'I'm in engineering'; 'I am in marketing in the car industry'. In fact, as the interview process continued down through from junior to middle management, the range of responses varied even more.

Such examples appear unimportant were it not for the fact that an accurate corporate positioning statement is not just important in marketing terms and how employees talk about the organisation externally, it is important because an accurate positioning statement reflects company culture, style, ethical principles, and the embodiment of the life and standards of an organisation. More importantly it will reflect the strategic priorities of the chief executive. For this reason one of the most important questions we put to CEOs and their chairmen during any corporate positioning analysis is: 'Where do you see the company's position in five or ten years' time?'

A leader's personal vision is important because it reflects an organisation's response to concerns about how global business will respond to the changes we discussed earlier. In the preparation of a satisfactory positioning statement, a response to such questions need clearly defining well in advance of the pressures that may take hold of world business in the years ahead because it will be too late for a company response if change is already occurring.

A Positioning Methodology

What are the most effective methodologies available for an organisation if the intention is to establish their likely positioning in the future? This process, frequently termed the 'communications audit' by public affairs practitioners, normally involves three stages. The ultimate aim is to develop a 'Statement' which embodies the elements within a company's existence. It is complex and will take many forms. The methodology described here is accepted by many management and communications practitioners because it has been applied by the authors to organisations ranging from global multinationals, medium-sized public-quoted companies, professional law and accountancy firms to creative service operations. Its credentials are well established. It has sufficient flexibility to be applied to any global organisation regardless of size, geography and cultural background. It can include in its respondent list for questioning in the first stage, which is soft data collection, a range of individual stakeholders even within the companies which themselves influence and impact the primary stakeholders.

The objective then of the audit is to develop a statement reflecting the real company and not the often inaccurate views and beliefs of its Board of Directors or trustees. This is an important factor as the respect in which an organisation is held affects the acceptability of its message. Having completed a programme of perhaps 30–40 interviews within the country of primary activity, the second phase is how that assembled data can become the traction for an overarching list of two to three alternative strategies ready for presentation to the Board of Directors or trustees. Each strategy must stand on its own and offer a potential description of the company culture and the valid messages the organisation can safely project to its matrix of stakeholders, of which the global public is an important ingredient. It can be a useful precursor if each strategy offered is tested as to its viability in terms of converting the abstract ideas into reality. Will each of the suggested strategies stand up to assessment by a corporate relations team vested with the task of creating an implementation programme? If the programme is developed over an agreed timeframe what are the chances of it achieving positive research results?

Having presented the alternative positioning strategies to management and obtained one agreed positioning, the task is to prepare a programme of activity to project that statement to an established and agreed list of target stakeholders. Before developing a memorable positioning for an institution such as an international multinational corporation (MNC), the audit methodology will hopefully assume the Herculean task of clearing the Aegean Stables, a task more complex and time-intensive than many Board directors understand. Despite the importance and difficulty of developing an accurate positioning for a company it is important to discuss the belief that a Board of Directors can formulate a positioning statement internally using a task force composed of internal managers and directors. Multinational operations have been identified above because size matters in terms of influencing community and business change. They are the influential players.

It should be emphasised that methodologies discussed in this book are applicable to any size or type of organisations. Our immediate concern however is with the large 'Fortune 500-type companies because they are the institutions that affect global attitudes and ensure the changes discussed in our earlier chapters can progress.

The establishment of a positioning statement for an organisation which can be projected and remembered constitutes a reputation builder. It is, as we have said, a three-part process assembling data from the alternative strategies and suitable as a provider of traction for a programme of activity that will achieve certain objectives for the creation of an external reputation. Positioning for any organisation will enable a statement to be prepared that will describe the product(s), the target audience or stakeholder, and the philosophy which drives corporate culture. It is the last of these three elements that concern us. It is the element which requires the individual attention of the chief executive because it is there that the differentiation from competitors is generated. Bearing in mind that an effective positioning statement should be no longer than four or five paragraphs, it can still take many hours to complete. It will be pregnant with meaning and devoid of sloganising. It will provide the gold seam from which material is prepared for internal and external audiences, chairmen's speeches and annual reports, employee newsletters, media statements and briefing documents for advertising agencies. All of these will be derived not necessarily in the exact words but through the inherent meaning of a 'Positioning Statement'.

It is our experience that although many, if not the majority, of large companies consider they have a coherent communications strategy, very few have one that dictates the essence and wording of a single positioning. The form of words must ensure all its stakeholders see, remember and absorb the same message. The message becomes the personality of the company in the mind of its publics. It is a behavioural and cultural essence which provides the response to the challenge set by the Director of the Financial Conduct Authority quoted earlier and other bodies such as the Confederation of British Industry (CBI) and The Institute of Directors which all help refute the public criticisms of a private enterprise economy. It will go further than this. It will establish an all-pervading positioning. The process is lengthy, taking time and effort, but getting it right and generating a memorable corporate reputation is the vehicle through which everything suggested in this book can be achieved.

Implementing the New Positioning

Although the methodology described draws together three strands:

1.   data research;

2.   positioning strategy; and

3.   communications theory,

it must underpin the final implementation programme. There can be a fourth stage, which is the monitoring of the results among target groups within the stakeholder universe. Quantitative research is more useful if carried out at six-monthly intervals and correlated with questions on financial economic and general business infrastructure identified on and off-line to identify which elements of the message appear to be reaching which sectors of each target cohort.

Returning to stage one of the methodologies, which can be described as the assembling of data from which the strategy is to evolve, we are frequently asked, what should be the size of the respondent base for the positioning? The phrase 'assembling the data' is used because it describes a function which is strictly qualitative research, but it does not necessarily abide by the rules of textbook qualitative research. The methodology is a series of one-on-one, face-to-face interviews working against an agreed topic menu. Sometimes the quantitative data already exists as it has been assembled for a different purpose. This can provide useful inputs but the data may be out of date especially if carried out for FMCG (fast moving consumer goods) products or even more inaccurate if derived from discussions concerning governmental relations. What is important is to clearly define the information required before starting. Every case is different but the end objective is to gain internal insights into departmental human relations and the interrelations between the staff and their systems before establishing any omnibus strategies. This should include the interaction between departments and their management style in terms of human relations. How are new ideas encouraged and discipline imposed in regard to time keeping and adherence to intellectual property control? The information-gathering phase against a topic menu is itself modular, with functional breakdowns and sections inserted to encourage supplementary questions that can be a response to previous replies.

To assess variations of opinion within an organisation regarding how employees view the company and how they describe externally its function and positioning early on in the research process, it can be useful to start, as we explained earlier, interview sessions with the open-ended question: 'When you are in a social situation and asked what your job is, how do you reply?'

If the answer is simple such as: 'I am an accountant or designer', it can lead into a supplementary question as to: 'What does that job entail?' If a friendly, easy atmosphere is maintained throughout the interview process the respondent can be encouraged to talk about the company, its customer base and general reputation in the first stage of the interview. If left until later the respondent's mind has already moved forward and developed a fresh set of emotional responses. These can, and usually do, influence later discussion and stimulate even more detailed questions.. If used in the early stages of the interview process, the discussion can remain open ended and it may be an effective moment to move into a standard SWOT (Strengths, Weaknesses, Opportunities and Threats) formula. In any case it is a useful process as it sets replies into priority order. It provides soft data by the end of the audit process but also, by assembling such priorities, it leads naturally into questions concerning the organisation's structure and may forecast comments that reflect the over-arching ability of the organisation to respond to industry change.

It is important that interviewers (possibly accompanied by a colleague) should encourage wide comment but never ever become involved in the discussion and never voice an opinion. This is a skill that experienced interviewers learn. This ability is gained through experience and it should widen the discussion to generate additional information sometimes outside the strict rigour of the topic menu. The interviewer should never allow the interview to become a conversation. As one psychologist once remarked to this author (RW) in describing the process of quantitative research, it should be an adventure not a recipe. The order in which subjects are discussed is important. A reply generated too early in the session can affect how the respondent views later questions. Sometimes it is advisable to ask the same question later but in a different format so answers are still valid but are not immediately seen as a repeat question. This can be an important approach if respondents are asked their business reading habits, especially regarding business journals and financial magazines. Without being unduly cynical there is a tendency for ambitious junior respondents to respond with answers they believe will impress their senior managers. By putting a question differently or asking about article subjects it is easy to assess a respondent's actual reading habits.

If the organisation under review already has an external relations programme, the audit and its accompanying topic menu should be continued but with an external audit. This will consist of similar interview questions put to business and academic leaders or opinion formers within the same industry. It can include interviews with government representatives at a national and international level, with local authority leaders and perhaps with appropriate leaders within a wider global business infrastructure not involved in the same industry. In some cases it is possible to obtain the names of middle to senior managers who have left the company and who, along with new recruits, can also be useful and can answer questions on the impression they gained of their company's culture and its different style of decision making as a newcomer.

It is important to undertake audits of the type described with experienced interviewers whose experience is not in traditional market research. The skills required for a corporate audit are similar to those of management consultancy. The interviewer will know what is to be achieved but will be sufficiently restrained to avoid wider discussion. It is important that the interviewer has studied and analysed existing data within the company before involvement in one-on-one interviews. There is normally an Aladdin's Cave of information and data within a company which has been forgotten or is not seen as being of interest for research.

The past 12–24 months' media coverage (hard copy television and online), not to forget in-house newsletters, should all be read, analysed and assembled into a chronological and phraseological matrix. Print material such as annual reports, sales brochures and house journals within each SBU can be assessed using the type of semiotic assessment described in the previous chapter. A brochure or internal house magazine projects syntagms or items of information as described earlier, and these leave messages within the reader's mind which may not have been intended by the director of corporate relations or indeed by the sign-writer. On the theme of corporate relations, it is tactful to establish contact with the internal department head and any external consultants already appointed for implementation. The style of contact must vary according to the instructions originally determined by the CEO when commissioning the analysis. In some cases the positioning study has been commissioned precisely because the CEO is unsure about the effectiveness or professionalism of the functions implementation and the reasons for the study can only be discussed with the commissioning chief executive.

If the interviewer completes the above analysis before any actual interviews it will guide the process with sufficient background to drive supplementary questions and provide a deeper understanding of responses.

The Topic Menu

The topic menu is an important tool in the process because it is not a traditional questionnaire nor is it a list of general questions. It has a broad structure of questions and is often divided by function after the initial questions have been completed. Even so they must maintain enough flexibility to allow supplementary questions that may not even refer to that module of the audit. What is important is that the same topic menu is used for every interview whether it is internal or external. This does not mean the responses can be treated quantitatively. If traditional market research criteria are to be used the positioning analysis edges towards qualitative research but should not be seen as such for the reasons described. Any final assembling of responses will be by all interviewers who, as we have said, must be experienced interviewers treating the analysis with intellectual subjectivity.

As stated, every respondent should be asked the same opening question: 'How do you describe the organisation informally when asked by an external or indeed internal contact, whether they are professional business or simply at some social event?' The intention is to gain a front of mind response before the respondent has moved into 'interview mode'. One of the reasons why the topic menu is never sent to the respondent ahead is to prevent considered answers which are frequently pregnant with baggage relating to the respondent's hidden agenda.

The most difficult element of soft data collection is avoiding respondents giving replies to questions they think the interviewer will want to hear, or in the case of internal interviews, what they consider their senior managers want to hear. Despite the fact that all respondents are informed that the replies to questions will not be identified by name, few respondents feel confident that their views will not become known to managers in the company.

The topic menu is divided into a series of areas that can range through functions such as technical/manufacturing/research, marketing, media relations, human resources or other areas the management or industry sector signifies. If the interviewer is accompanied by a colleague, strict rules must be maintained in the sense that no discussion should take place after an individual interview is finished. This is to avoid early opinions being created that will psychologically affect the attitude of the interviewer to later interviews, or worse, will affect subjectively the final assembly and interpretation of the total set of responses. This is an important regulation and one which is frequently ignored. We have said that the lead interviewer should be accompanied by a colleague. This is not essential but most interviewers find it helpful to have someone alongside also completing the topic menu, or if necessary helping to assess non-verbal gestures and respondent facial expressions.

Decisions as to the total number of interviews undertaken is difficult to advise. They vary according to function, availability of stakeholders and subjective opinions held by the organisation about individual managers and whether or not they represent a significant view within the corporate culture. It is important to remember the operation is not quantitative research in the sense that the percentage of answers to questions is not significant. The process is directed by the interviewer to create a relatively accurate understanding of the issues affecting the company.

On completion of the early stages of data collection through interview responses, the construction of the replies will be dependent on the boundaries set for the interviews. Sometimes it is only possible to range across a single country because of budget availability or if interviews are restricted to attendance at regional conferences by overseas managers at the right level of seniority. Sometimes interviews will be carried out in different regions using local interviewers. Decisions have to be made by the audit manager. Frequently they are taken according to data received. If there is a consistency of responses there may be no need for extra validation. If there are atypical responses it may be due to choosing a respondent who is already known to be a maverick and who has built a reputation for rocking the boat due to their own prejudices. In some cases it may be necessary to put extra questions to validate or not the majority of responses on that subject. In terms of geography it may be necessary to involve external consultants respected in selected regions.

The aim is to develop a positioning statement which describes clearly what the organisation does, for whom and the philosophy that drives it. What is important for the future is to ensure that questions concerning the communications and possibly involvement of the organisation with individual stakeholders have been included in the topic menu for each stakeholder because those responses will affect later decisions regarding a programme of activities within the business community. This could underpin the organisation's reputation. The process of asking about such involvement plays an important role in stimulating directors to realise their own lacunae in terms of working with the community within which the organisation operates. If the questions are well defined they are by implication suggesting activities the company should be considering. It is often more effective to ask if a company is involved in certain functions within the community rather than suggest directly that they become involved.

The importance of writing an accurate positioning statement cannot be understated. Its accuracy is important in terms of making managers realise where the company stands at that moment in terms of reputation, thus establishing guide lines for change. This is basic and many companies realise what action is needed in terms of improving their external reputation among certain publics but have not taken action to implement change. By identifying the fact there is a public relations need, it may be seen as a technical communications failure whereby certain stakeholder publics are being omitted from the wider programme. There may be a false understanding of the company's management intentions. This can be put right through traditional communications techniques such as media exposure, event organisation, sponsorship, online social media or even direct marketing to those audiences that can be reached by the most efficient delivery system for that particular message. Most organisations turn to external consultants and brief them to provide and implement a programme to counter such problems because they bring to bare a more accurate sense of objectivity.

More usually the audit process identifies the need to establish and refresh the external reputation to meet changes in the business environment. Frequent causes of reputation problems are mergers, acquisitions of other companies, changes in the product range or expansion into new markets. The inclusion of all stakeholder groups in the list of respondents for interview is probably the most useful addition to normal market research processes. It sets building blocks for a company to meet the changes forecast in this book. Any organisation that shows negative responses to questions concerning interrelationships or lack of close involvement with stakeholders such as suppliers, advisers, government officials (local, national or international), involvement in industry bodies or institutions within their industry infrastructure will know that they have an immediate need to remove that negative situation. They will need to develop a policy of total involvement if they are to be ready for the intensification of new public and government pressures in the years ahead.

The Way Forward

We are already identifying the changes we forecast in the way ahead for businesses and organisations as they edge forward into what is in effect a new era. Such changes are a response to what Professor Michael Porter, along with Dr Mark R. Kramer, of Harvard Business School, say in the *Harvard Business Review* (Porter and Kramer, 2011) when he claims that:

> *The capitalist system is under siege. In recent years business increasingly has been viewed as a major cause of social, environmental and economic*

problems. Companies are widely perceived to be prospering at the expense of the broader community. Even worse, the more business has begun to embrace corporate responsibility, the more it has been blamed for society's failures. The legitimacy of business has fallen to levels not seen in recent history. This diminished trust in business leads political leaders to set policies that undermine competitiveness and sap economic growth. Business is caught in a vicious circle. A big part of the problem lies with companies themselves, which remain trapped in an outdated approach to value creation that has emerged over the past few decades. They continue to view value creation narrowly, optimizing short-term performance in a bubble while missing the most important customer needs and ignoring the broader influences that determine their longer term success.

Porter goes on to say in the *Harvard Business Review* that

... companies must take the lead in bringing business and society back together. The recognition is there among sophisticated businesses and thought leaders, and promising elements of a new model are emerging. Yet we still lack an overall framework for guiding these efforts, and most companies remain stuck in a social responsibility mind-set in which societal issues are at the periphery, not the core.

The corporate audit as described above lays a foundation to move, as Porter suggests, into a new era. The development of a positioning for any organisation establishes a base, where our earlier chapters discussing stakeholder values, ethical business and stakeholder dialogues lay the objectives that any organisation should consider if it is sensitive to the strictures set out above.

There is a growing belief, and it is likely to gather pace, about involvement. This is not involvement in a loose sense of round table talking shops but involvement in terms of genuinely helping stakeholder companies to improve their management and move their operations into success mode on their own terms. Many companies lean heavily on suppliers and force down prices regardless of the impact the income reduction will have on the supplier's bottom line.

Professor Porter calls this 'creating shared values'. What is interesting is that we are seeing the early stages of sharing goals in other areas such as government and third world relations. The principle of involvement is not new. For many years in UK town planning legislation there has been a legislative item called

Section 106, more recently extended as the Community Infrastructure Levy (CIL). The purpose of Section 106, and then CIL, is to allow local government authorities to demand a contribution by major developers to improve the surrounding physical environment. What started as an opportunity through Section 106 for local government to draw down significant sums of money proportionate to the total cost of the development to improve highways, develop education services, build community halls or simply improve the look of highway furniture, was extended in the UK in April 2010 by the CIL above with wider options to build and develop community services such as museums, new roads, parks and even buy public art. This combined approach to output improvement when permission is given for large, and now even smaller, development projects has been slow to take off in every urban area or local authority. This is especially so if the political persuasion of the authority is opposed.

The concept is the first sign of the beginning of something larger in different situations. For example, the UK Government Cabinet Minister responsible for International Development at the time of writing is Justine Greening, a Conservative MP. Greening is a Chartered Accountant with a MBA from a UK business school, and was appointed by the Prime Minister, David Cameron, to control global overseas aid. It was seen at first as a downgrade, where all that was required would be a hand out of funds to third world countries, almost a charity giving appointment. In fact the Minister applied a business mind to the problem. It was reported that she took a group of UK companies to Tanzania. She was not asking them to give money, usually the first request in the past with Ministers in this role – she decided that Tanzania was to be a testing ground for a trial in which her department would lend money to businesses rather than give traditional grant aid. Tanzania and four other African counties have been chosen as economic partners with the UK in regions where British expertise matched the local needs. The other partner countries were Mozambique, Ghana, Angola and Ivory Coast. The decision was to cut red tape making it easier to trade with the region.

The London Stock Exchange will also help to develop capital markets. By putting in its own cash, the Government reduces its partner's risk of losing money and it is hoped that this will help attract investment. Greening claims that 'the move will benefit the wealth in some of the most unequal countries in the world this is not about bringing back tied aid' where countries in the past received British aid and were forced to buy British products. The initiative is about finding new markets that will in themselves attract more investments and move into a second-level economic development.

This concept, if understood correctly, can become a wider programme whereby large multinational companies become involved with their stakeholders, not necessarily through the investment of funds, although this might happen, but for the investment of skills. Many suppliers, especially at the SME level, need help in terms of improving their own financial controls, marketing their products to other buyers and calling on their hub company to provide high-standard training skills.

On first sight it may appear to be a campaign to give money. In fact it is the opposite. Stakeholder companies can improve their own management, improve their bottom line and maintain profits that can be reinvested in NPD which can help their hub company. The overall concept requires a total reconsideration of the business supplier/demand sale within the hub companies' stakeholders which can, if well developed, result in cross-investment and sales between individual stakeholder and general cooperation. Historically there had been some interaction between companies, NGOs and large international organisations. An article in *The Economist* (2013b) commented that they

> ... *have become like off-site team-building exercises: they were once slightly exotic, but now no self-respecting firm does without them. A survey of European multinationals and British charities by C&E Advisory Services found that over a third of the firms invest £10m or more in their charitable alliances and almost two-thirds classify the partnerships as 'strategic'.*

This is a view that underpins the argument we discussed earlier (Chapter 2) that 'ethical business is sustainable business'. *The Economist* article, however, goes on to say that 'these partnerships are partnerships of opposites ... businesses tend to think they discharge their duty to society by obeying the law'. Businesses think in terms of markets, not rights, and most companies sign up for such schemes to look good whether or not the activity is worthwhile. Some critics of this approach believe such shows of individual involvement only look good and that the way forward is worldwide central planning. This view is expressed on the left of British politics, but since the post-war government policies of nationalised industry and services has now lost its bloom because bitter experience of the last few decades has shown that London's central government, known as Whitehall, does not always know best, and the closer macro schemes can be directed by competent managers as described in our positioning analysis, the more likely objectives in terms of helping those in need can be achieved.

Just as *The Economist* article maintains, companies can provide money, which all charities need. They also offer a way of influencing the behaviour of millions. The same can be said about close personal involvement by large companies with their variety of suppliers and services. We have been concerned in this chapter with the process by which chief executives who support the frequently heard cry in the media from young people that 'business must step up' and remove the historic barriers between success in bottom-line business terms and becoming involved in societal values in a more interactive model. Porter and Kramer's paper (2011) continues the views we argue that, for profit-oriented businesses, it is in their own interest and that of society to develop a new bicultural orientation. They argue too that companies must take the lead in bringing business and society back together. They say that 'a growing number of companies known for their hardnosed approach to business such as GE, Google, IBM, Intel, Nestle and Unilever have already embarked on important efforts to create shared value by reconceiving the intersection between society and corporate performance'. They continue in their paper, demanding that governments should learn to regulate their ways to enable shared value rather than work against it. They consider that capitalism is an unparalleled vehicle for meeting human needs, improving efficiency, creating jobs and building wealth. But a narrow conception of capitalism has prevented business from harnessing its full potential to meet society's broader challenges, that businesses acting as businesses not as charitable donors are the most powerful force for addressing the pressing needs we face. The moment for a new conception of capitalism is now. Society's needs are large and growing, they say. In fact they argue that 'perhaps most important of all, learning how to create shared value is our best chance to legitimize business again', not see such non-profit activities as an irresponsible use of shareholders' money. As we titled Chapter 2: 'Ethical Business is Sustainable Business'. In fact, as Porter's paper argues, strengthening the local clusters of supporting suppliers and other institutions can and should increase the efficiency of the total corporate constituency within which it operates. Porter explains that a business needs a successful community, not only to create demand for its products, but to provide a critical public asset. The concept he supports is that shared value can be defined as policies and operating practices that embrace competitiveness of a company while simultaneously advancing the economic and social conditions in the communities within which it operates and that shared value creation focuses on identifying and expanding the connection between societal and economic progress.

Strategy theory holds that to be successful a company must create a distinctive value proposition that meets the needs of a chosen set of customers.

As argued earlier, the positioning analysis as a methodology takes differentiation from all other companies as one of the audit's objectives. The concept of shared value resets the boundaries of capitalism by better connecting companies' success with societal improvement. The ability to create shared value applies equally to advanced economies and developing countries though the specific opportunities differ. It is the objective of any organisations' leader over the next few years to strive to achieve this concept of the shared success.

Summary

1. Establishing a memorable corporate positioning is a CEO's first priority. It takes time, budget and commitment. Without it other strategies will fail in the upcoming business climate.

2. New capitalism must be about shared values and a close personal involvement with a bicultural orientation by senior managers with their stakeholders.

3. The best companies are building into their positioning: cultures and communications, the wishes and expectations of the full range of all their stakeholders and sometimes even their stakeholder's stakeholders.

4. Capitalism is an unparalleled vehicle for meeting human needs, improving efficiency, and creating jobs and wealth, but only if its current narrow concept is widened to achieve real shared values. Business and society must be brought together.

PART IV
Lifelong Learning and Knowledge Sharing

Chapter 7

Willingly to School

In the play *As You Like It*, the English poet and playwright William Shakespeare refers to the seven ages of man, of which the first is having to go 'unwillingly to school'. It is our view the opposite is the case for business leaders. They should be lifelong students, ready, regardless of their hierarchical success, to learn from attending business courses and reading academic papers that do not immediately appear to have relevance. In fact when Tom Peters, the US management writer, said some years ago that successful chief executives dedicated half their working day to reading books, he was only partly joking, as we argue in this chapter.

In Chapter 5 we emphasised the leadership skills that will become increasingly important in the years ahead. We were referring primarily to managers who want to hit the high ground running. That high ground could be heading up a public company quickly or becoming a manager, rising more slowly through the ranks of a NGO or perhaps leading a global-sized charity. Whatever the size or type of organisation, the skills needed are almost the same. An emphasis on strategy will increasingly be in demand for the higher leadership functions.

The exception can be those appointments where leadership is within a business unit closely directed by a group head office. Strategy, in such cases, has to embrace the requirements of an all-embracing conglomerate policy that may or may not maintain complex control systems across the business units. It is irrelevant whether their objective is to grow the financial bottom line or simply use their appointment to impact the wider community.

As the Editor of the *Times Higher Education* journal remarked (2013):

> *We are entering an era in which demand for world class education will be supercharged by the next generation of emerging economies with the now ubiquitous BRICS (Brazil, Russia, India, China, and South Africa) challenged by a group of young pretenders called the MINTs:*

Mexico, Indonesia, Nigeria, and Turkey. Various factors have put these economies on the front foot but demographics are still the key. The MINT's youthful populations will need to achieve the highest levels of business education if they are to maximise productivity and compete with the world's successful economies.

In this chapter we carry our argument forward with the emphasis on the 'how to' and 'where' process.

Every skill we discuss is applicable and although there was less time devoted in earlier chapters to training middle managers, most of the ingredients will be the same. So far there has been no specific discussion on training for start-up entrepreneurs wanting to build their own businesses because those skills are the same as those for the ambitious leader aiming to hit the top of an established operation. Many business schools are reporting over 20 per cent of their graduates have decided to launch their own start-up. The advice we give recent graduates, whatever the degree level, is to aim to work first in a high-calibre operation for five years before going it alone. Experience gained early or immediately after business school at the work face is invaluable when it comes to starting a new operation. There is nothing like learning about mistakes at someone else's expense.

The media frequently describe cases of millionaires who either skipped going to university or started a specialist company in a field they knew well. We argue they are the proverbial exceptions that prove the rule. Their worlds are not separate and no one launching their own company should reject advice on the basis that 'such business theory is for the big guys. I will be a mini for many years before I need absorb high-level management training'.

Leadership of global charities, for example, is an area where the leadership qualities and methodologies of leadership are still applicable and it is good to see data now appearing which shows charitable social organisations being listed as an important objective for enrolment on MBA courses.

It is interesting that another role for MBA training is described in an article in *The Sunday Times* (2013) written by Carly Chynoweth. She quotes a 48-year-old student who works in fund raising saying to her:

Getting the MBA gave me an insight into how people who work in business talk and think, which has made it easier for me to build relationships with potential donors ... now when I approach them I can

*say 'you should collaborate with us because there will be these benefits
for your company' rather than 'please give us money to do good work'.*

The chance to build ties between sectors, says Carly Chynoweth, is one reason business schools are keen to encourage applicants from charities, social enterprises and other not-for-profit organisations.

Simon Learmount, Director of the Executive MBA programme at Cambridge University Judge Business School in the UK, supports this view saying: 'Students from the voluntary sector are a valuable addition to courses. It is advantageous for all participants to develop breadth of experience by interacting with people from a variety of backgrounds.'

The MBA Syllabus: A Time for Change

The emphasis in this chapter is concerned with business education as a provider of tools that will oil the escalator to success. Business education is high visibility at this time and, as we explain, rapid changes can be expected from today (2014) forward, especially with the impact of MOOCs interacting with multi-country university syllabuses.

Emma Boyde, writing in the *Financial Times* Business Education Supplement (2013e) under the heading 'The Long View', considers 'a shake-out is coming which will force MBA programmes to focus on what they should be doing,' which is putting emphasis on quality, because employers will more and more demand an ability to work across cultures. She quotes B-school deans who are underwhelmed at what we tend to call distance learning. This includes the British Open University courses and MOOCs. They maintain that employers are less impressed by people who have degrees from such courses rather than the intense emotional and academic results obtained through face-to-face learning with lecturers and fellow students. They stress the importance of social competence and the fact that distance learning does not prepare people to be 'fantastic colleagues but only fantastic analysts'. We are unsure about the validity of such criticism and, as we commented earlier, MOOCs may be able to offer a broadening opportunity for companies to train significantly more staff than through traditional in-house schemes and should not be dismissed out of hand. Horses for courses.

Journalist Emma Boyde, however, quotes Professor Chambers, the MBA director at the University of Oxford's Said Business School, who says 'the MBA of the future needs to train people you will want to work with. Courses should support the movement towards greater corporate responsibility while at the same time preparing students to deal with' what he calls 'unparalleled global risks such as water shortages, pandemics and food problems'. He points out for example that 'students must also be able to find a home for a wall of global capital seeking a new asset class'. He argues that if the MBA ends up looking like a philosophy degree then fine.

The above article closes by quoting Professor Martha Maznevski, MBA programme Director at IMD Switzerland, and Professor O'Connor, Dean of Essec France that 'the focus on emerging nations is going to be an increasingly important differentiator and that Europeans are more used to managing diversity'.

Having quoted business school deans, unsure about the importance of distance learning because of employee attitudes, it is important to note that some academics and particularly journalists, who have tested a variety of MOOC MBAs, argue the variations in quality are significant and potential students should test the market as they would for the purchase of a house or holiday. Both play just as important a role in their lives. Some lecturers have quickly understood the difference between their traditional weekly lecture where they respond to audience reaction by face and body language and indeed deal with questions and subsidiary discussion with the MOOC lecturer to perhaps 200,000 students in different parts of the world and from a variety of cultural backgrounds.

In the plus column, MOOCs are free and the supporting text also low cost. The final reward may or may not be a degree, depending on related linkages or more likely a Certificate of Accomplishment collected by online involvement. In some cases courses are academic in style with lecturers simply placing their traditional material online, while others creatively design a range of environments and situations to enhance the spoken words. Some courses have the speaker tucked into the corner of the screen and the visuals filling the centre screen.

One element is sure, online MBA courses are in the kindergarten stage of what will become an increasingly important learning system affecting aspiring communities. Some members will be using MOOC lectures as launch pads for other courses, others as a reinvigorating opportunity for first-degree graduates. Such participants, because of their numbers, may influence employers in what they can demand from junior appointees. The division between traditional post-work experience MBA graduates along with pre-work graduates from Masters in Business degree courses and those who aspire to only junior positions, who start but fail to complete a full MOOC, will morph in both directions.

Education as Training

Training and business education is often rejected by SME owner–managers on the grounds of 'no budget'. Yet strangely it is usually small companies that gain the most from a commitment to staff training. This author (RW) has experience as a non-executive director with many small companies. One of my first requests to the chief executive of an SME after my appointment is that a morning a week (usually Mondays) should be turned over to an hour's training. It requires total commitment by the owner–manager and the generation of an attitude within the company whatever its size, that getting better at their job is important for all employees as well as for the company's reputation externally. It is important to set out a programme well ahead with subjects identified as being obviously (to them) useful for every level of staff in their day-to-day work. The issues discussed in the training sessions can become important vehicles for moulding company culture. More importantly, for the changes we expect in the future, a flexible weekly training programme can prepare staff for new issues that social pressure will demand of them.

What form then should the training take? It can be no more than informal discussion on professional methodologies or hearing presentations by supplier companies who want to put their own skills across, or leaders from trade association and professional bodies interested in presenting to employees who may buy their skills. They are all potential presenters on in-house training programmes. One of the clichés I use in such presentations is that 'small companies must think like big companies'. The skills tool box is the same. But even a single hour in-house training each week adds up (if attendance is compulsory) to 50 hours training a year – more than staff in companies that pay high fees for two- to three-week full-time courses.

Entrepreneurial Success

The DO School, based in Hamburg and founded by Entrepreneur Florian Hoffman who developed the school, offers budding entrepreneurs a chance to develop new product ideas. Sixty students are chosen each year from formal applications often sponsored by their country's governments, or by a charity or philanthropist. The DO Schools are based in many places but are particularly successful at their London and New York venues. The students, however, come from countries all over the globe and return to their countries at different times in their course as they learn basic skills. The aim is to educate the next generation of leaders in the hope they will eventually make a global impact. There is a growing plethora of such global training organisations now in place to help young entrepreneurs. The intention is to impart the skills the students would learn if they had sufficient financial support to enrol in formal business school courses and degrees of the type discussed earlier.

On the same theme *The Times* interviewed ten young students whose success stories suggested it is not always necessary to attend business school to make a start-up product idea work. The intention of the research interviews was to find their secrets despite the fact they had swept to success on their own terms notwithstanding the comments we made earlier. None of the respondents went to business school or graduated from university with an MBA or business degree.

The success factors were remarkably similar: gather the right people (recruitment styles and methodologies were important), and their products had to be marketed with professional skill. Respondents claimed they had to manage cash flow carefully (57 per cent cited this as a significant factor). Others said they delayed entry into new markets until their second year (too soon takes the eye off the basics). They all had a clear strategy which although flexible was detailed and contained no generalisations. One said 'avoid being a one hit wonder and concentrate on a small group of effective activities'. Others stressed the importance of building a strong financial base to provide a safety net if sales fall for uncontrollable reasons such as economic downturns, and finally, don't rush. Throughout the interviews one factor was constant: 'get the right people around you'.

Interviewing is not always an effective way to make people choices. Checking testimonials is important as is the need to prolong the interviewing process using examples that will test candidate reactions. Where possible however, it is important to have a trusted colleague sharing the selection process. Certainly never make a decision on one, or even two interviews. People selection is a skilled business and paper qualifications are not necessarily an effective guide to judging character traits such as loyalty, energy and willingness to work long hours. Above all, assess whether a certain personality will fit in with other existing colleagues.

Global Business Training

Working in harmony is a fundamental factor on the road to success in small companies. Effective business education depends on a flexible response to business change and if the financial resources are there and the students can afford to take an MBA course it will build on core skills by injecting globally oriented response to business change. The rigidity of many business school courses can result in students failing to appreciate changes in the business environment of the type we discussed earlier.

One example is the important role of online and off-line communications at global rather than national level. If business schools are to train students to achieve senior management appointments at its highest level then they need to stand back and consider the range of subjects needed for top leadership positions regardless of the continuing debate on course lengths. Some courses are already demanding a pre-course week or two weeks to underpin later skills training. One area that is seldom considered, regardless of where the courses are aimed, is the growing importance of creating an understanding of the meeting of minds between business and government policy making. Mark Esposito, Associate Professor at Grenoble Ecole de Management, writing in the *Financial Times* (2013g) is concerned at the way business careers and politics are treated as being separate. He says although 'business schools have argued for the introduction of interdisciplinary courses … business education remains trapped in the same business model that has been around for the past 30 years'. The business mindset can be brought into public policy. In the years to come business and civil society will have to recognise that the previous models of the world no longer work and adapt accordingly.

At the other extreme, this author (RW), involved over many years in local and national government policy making, has been surprised at the ignorance of senior business executives of the fundamentals of how governments operate. On many occasions clients have said they were working at the top level to achieve a decision with their local authority and invited the local Mayor to lunch, not realising that, apart from those cities and boroughs in the UK and other countries which have directly elected decision-making Mayors, it is the leader of the majority party who takes decisions not their Mayors. The same applies to national government where a chief executive meets a Cabinet Minister socially and expects to telephone afterwards for further policy shaping discussion. A meeting is set up and the CEO is shocked to find the Minister is accompanied by three or four officials for every subsequent meeting and every comment is recorded.

The MBA as a Cornerstone?

At one time the MBA degree, which has been one of the academic successes of the last two decades, was seen as a motorway to success in large multinational companies. A growing number of students set their sights, before they completed their courses, on a desire to found and build their own company. If they manage to enrol on a business school Master's degree like an MBA, they graduate as well-seasoned managers one or two steps ahead of those who launched into the business arena from a virgin start. This is because they had the chance to analyse other companies and learn from their mistakes. Before moving into advanced areas of, for example, transcribing academic theories that are unlikely to have been considered for normal management practice, future leaders should have established their business school credentials to build a foundation for leadership.

The MBA was first offered by Harvard Business School back in 1908. It conquered the US quickly but it was not until after the Second World War that it really reached Europe at the French Business School INSEAD who launched it in 1957. More recently, universities across the globe, not to mention local business schools, have tended to offer it as an important product for the ambitious manager. In the UK, the London and Manchester Business Schools were the first to take it on board and they have both settled down as two of the top in the world. Because courses are constructed to encourage positive response to change they are an important vehicle to help leaders capable of generating significant changes and respond, the type of new pressures we forecast for the coming decade.

What then is the background and changing demand for a business education? It is interesting that in 2013 there were four times more MBA graduates from US colleges than graduates with law degrees. India now has more than 1,000 business schools. China has approximately 250 MBA programmes and 30,000 business students. In Chapter 5, discussing the lifestyle and social mores of the 18–49 age group, we commented that demand for high salaries is not so apparent globally as previously. Business schools now consider their graduates are less concerned than they once were about earning fabulous salaries. Business schools reel off (in their marketing brochures) examples of those who joined non-profit operations or launch social enterprises. Most business schools are now encouraging students to concentrate on one area, such as finance or health, and many courses are tailored to particular industries.

There are, of course, dangers in graduating with one specialist industry in mind when the purpose of the MBA course is to encourage a fundamental but wider rethink on student careers. It is important when considering the changes we forecast for the decade ahead to realise that business training should instruct and train senior managers for whatever changes take place in the later decades of a middle manager's life. One of the most useful influences in this formative stage is the influence of educational technology and the evolving power, as we said earlier, of the Massive Online Open Courses (MOOCs). Some deans are unsure about the full impact of these courses but from the student viewpoint they will become increasingly influential, as they are more user friendly. As we have said, there are only a few MBAs currently offered on MOOCs but the future trends are there and we can expect a massive increase in business management courses in the coming years. Managers who feel left behind by colleagues will have refined their own skills. More likely, students have assimilated academic theories of the type discussed below. The changing products on offer at business schools make decision making by students more and more difficult regardless of whether it is a case of wait and see.

The Masters in Management degree is becoming more popular for younger students who want to expand their business knowledge immediately after their first degree with a one-year course. Such degrees are becoming increasingly popular. The widening of the reach and content of business degrees is only the beginning of what will become significantly more developed. The Dean of the IEB Business School in Madrid predicts that new disciplines such as behavioural economics and cognitive psychology will find a home in the MBA curriculum. We agree with that diagnosis and describe later potential new management disciplines.

Successful managers need to understand the contexts and interrelationships that exist between different stakeholders and, by developing the right metrics and using that data to influence their decision making, they will identify the right message for the right audience. There is a communications chain which cascades within corporate structures. Some syllabuses aim to sensitise students to the internal and external pressures which influence decision making. One of the most frequent discussion questions asked by students globally, when they know we (the authors) have a connection with Henley Business School, is: What is included in the MBA syllabus at Henley (now a part of the University of Reading)? The interest is usually aroused because students from other universities want a comparison. For this reason we have listed in some detail below how Henley structures its MBA syllabus. What is termed

'The Henley Difference' in their MBAs, ensure seemingly unrelated disciplines are sufficiently integrated to:

- strengthen core teaching areas concerned with organisational structure;

- management choice; and

- the creation of differentiation in an organisation's positioning.

They constitute the core of the current Henley MBA which is summarised in detail as:

Stage One:

Managing the organisation: context and involvement, behaviour and choice of tools, techniques and evaluation/analysis.

Managing people: performance scoping, impact of context and motivation, performance culture, coaching.

Managing process: systems and projects:

- Integrate operational management, information systems.

- Process mapping, value chains, capacity management.

- Quality processes, knowledge management.

Managing financial resources: financial literacy, micro-economics, cost analysis, market structure.

Stage Two:

Making choices:

- The global business environment:
  - identify drivers;
  - macro-economic;
  - ethics and sustainability;
  - social impact of business on society.

- Strategic marketing:
  - relationship building with stakeholders;
  - marketing communications;
  - electronic and mobile advertising/communications.

- Corporate finance and governance (finance centre relationships).

- Future strategies and direction:
  - resources and capabilities;
  - competition and collaboration.

Stage Three:

Making a difference:

- Managing change and leadership:
  - change architecture;
  - organisation development and growth.

- Reputation and relationships:
  - value creation;
  - research;
  - literature reviews;
  - stakeholder relationships.

- The management challenge.

Communication and external reputation has become a holistic and integrated process encompassing and influencing an organisation's planning and corporate strategy. It is mediated by stakeholders through a range of intra-relationships. Because of the changing business environment, global managers need additions to their fundamental training. There is a Henley MBA module in Stakeholder Management which has injected the disciplines with each item taught within a global context as:

1. corporate governance and transparency;

2. leadership and personal communication;

3. stakeholder engagement and their interrelationships;

4.   risk and crisis management;

5.   societal culture change and public diplomacy;

6.   sustainable business and CSR;

7.   corporate branding, e-commerce and the application of research
        and online social media;

8.   communications and perception theory;

9.   the influence scorecard and differentiation measurement.

The above breakdown of the Henley MBA can provide a useful comparison for business academics globally, but even here, as we explain later, there are areas where adjacent academic disciplines, not to mention stronger theoretical underpinning, could strengthen many sectors of the Henley MBA to help students meet the challenges of the up-coming decade.

Peter Brews, writing in the *Financial Times* (2012c) comments that: 'The best way to provide a truly global business education is through international alliances in which partners participate equally in the educational process. Yet despite the frequent heralding of alliances by business schools, successful programs of this kind are still relatively thin on the ground.'

Elements of such courses must include assessments of change in global business culture to discuss the importance of understanding what Richard E. Nisbett argues in *The Geography of Thought* (2003) that his research led him to – the conviction that two utterly different approaches to thought between the global 'East' and global 'West' hemispheres have maintained themselves for thousands of years and they generate profoundly different social relations and views about thought processes. Such variant attitudes bear heavily on the way different audiences respond to the same corporate message. Through case studies and the expansion of their business focus, students are encouraged to acquire theoretical and applied knowledge of their disciplines to assess change within the global business infrastructure. An MBA's flexibility is essential if it is to appeal to the now-changing profile of typical MBA students.

No longer is an MBA on its own a guarantee of success, as Ross Tieman says in the *Financial Times* (2012b), quoting from the CEO of the US Association of Management Consulting Firms: 'Recruiters can no longer focus on graduates of leading MBA programmes, talent is more diverse and scattered across thousands of academic institutions. The whole thing has become unbelievably complicated.' The recent UK Government White Paper, which is a formal discussion document, opens opportunities for professional and non-professional bodies to attain university accreditation. A Government White Paper is basically a monograph by means of which government Ministers (and their departments) can publicise fresh thinking without the need for actual legislation. In fact White Papers do not require parliamentary sanction although they may well be debated in the British Parliament.

Embracing Academia

Some MBAs offer significantly wider horizons for students through the identification of business change and the need for management training to include techniques such as public diplomacy, visual semiotics and a more sophisticated use of social media. There is a need therefore to undertake detailed research of market demand and students' preferred formats to embrace some of these new techniques.

An example of where business school training frequently omits necessary ingredients is the potential to reach out to adjacent academic disciplines that are seldom grasped as having business potential. One such academic discipline that immediately comes to mind is the area of visual semiotics or the science of visual communication and its analysis. An understanding of even its basic principles can provide a new tool box of techniques and methodologies that help in the reading of the visual as one might read the written word. An academic 'morphing' of the visual over the textual, in both corporate and small business management, can provide an advantage missed by management at many levels and in many allied functions from marketing to public relations and governmental publicity. Executives marginalise visual elements in their stakeholder management programmes leaving that to external designers. This omission can mean changes in management culture within different geographical regions are left to generate a variety of interpretations of a corporate written message.

There is a potential training opportunity for ambitious managers aiming for the heights if they widen their own curiosity and examine a range of adjacent academic disciplines that could be injected into their personal tool-kit. We discuss below semiotics as one such skill. There are many others ranging through neuropsychology, international diplomacy, psychologically-driven

interpersonal relations and many others. Such exploratory adventures can
be exciting but they need to be monitored carefully if they are transposed for
business use,

The *Financial Times* summarised the situation when it entitled an article
(2012a): 'MBAs Need a Richer Educational Framework'. Our objective in
this book is to consider and identify some such techniques which could be
applicable to the business arena. We have chosen semiotics as an example of
what we mean by embracing academic disciplines and injecting them into the
box of business tools. We have selected non-linguistic semiotic communication.
Perhaps the use of underutilised concepts such as social semiotics and CDA
could be claimed from their base in academia to fill such lacunae. There is,
in semiotics, a body of knowledge not previously considered relevant which
can be embraced and developed for use in day-to-day management. Reading
visual images by applying the academic techniques of semiotics is only one
approach waiting to be assimilated into business training. The concept has been
expanded by Kress and van Leeuwen (1996). In the preamble to their seminal
work *Reading Images* they comment: 'As we move from a culture dominated by
language to one in which visual literacy becomes increasingly important a tool-
kit is needed for the reading of images.'

An example of such concepts is discussed here when applied to corporate
print material and indeed anywhere where the visual is equivalent to the
written word – the annual report being a typical artefact where visual grammar
can play an important role. In the detailed discussion below we aim is to
reduce the subjective criteria by which most managers make visual decisions.
What we have included is not a final solution. Semiotics is a wide subject and
semiotic visual models transcribe (perhaps translates is a better word) only a
basic selection of semiotic concepts. They are the ones that can form the basis
for readers to develop a more rigorous technique suitable for application into
business practice. What is important is that although some semiotic writers
such as Roland Barthes (1993) and Judith Williamson (1978) have applied such
concepts to commercial subjects, they have been primarily used in advertising
with the concentration on support for the written element there, where it is
usually a slogan.

The discussion is concerned to explain visual meaning transfer within
a corporate context because stakeholder audiences range across the whole
community. The differences are important because of the variety of end users
and because the material under analysis in a business situation may well have
been requested by an investment analyst, a politician, a trade customer or

even an academic. The process of choice is a factor within a wider element of message transfer.

The use of the word 'sign-maker' in the text is used to describe the creative team which produces corporate material. It means more than just the managers in the public affairs function but external graphics designers and photographers as well. The objective is to identify the degree of certainty and probability by which corporate material reflects the needs of, for example, the Board of Directors. The methodologies discussed here aim to reduce the level of subjectivity that occurs when *visual* texts are signed off as a reflection of corporate objectives.

Epistemologically speaking, such analysis can only reduce the level of uncertainty – it cannot remove it. This reductionist approach focuses the attention of business practitioners on small but discrete elements within a process. The micro elements may be as important in message delivery as the more obvious macro factors. The sign-maker usually concentrates on narrowly defined items. As a result managers are forced to concentrate in their preparation on the meaning of each item in the visual process.

Semiotics as a word derives from the lectures of the Swiss linguist Ferdinand de Saussure, whose ideas were published posthumously at the turn of the twentieth century by a group of students and staff, based upon his lectures. De Saussure (1966) said that 'a science that studies the life of signs within society is conceivable; it would be part of social psychology and consequently of general psychology: I shall call it semiology (from the Greek semion "sign"). Semiology would show what constitutes signs, what laws govern them'.

It is important to understand that by 'signs' we refer to all obvious versions such as those used in, say, the Highway Code or public signage. Semiotics refers to anything that can or might express meaning. Such marks or shapes even include writing (the letters CAT do not resemble a cat), pictures and overall design. They all constitute signs which are composed of a signifier and a signified and depending upon the closeness of the signifier to its meaning (which is arbitrary). It will need social acceptance by the decoders to increase in importance. Even visual texts must be analysed in terms of their meaning within a system of relationships.

The context defines the meaning and because there is no firm definition, meaning occurs by negotiation between reader and text. The Semiotic writer Barthes (1993) talked about the 'death of the author', that is, what the author writes has no firm meaning in itself (except to the author) but only in relation to how the reader interprets the written signs. These are mediated by their own discourse. As the Italian author and academic Umberto Eco says, people bring different codes to a message and therefore interpret it in different ways. Those codes have been assimilated and accepted as a result of social class, educational level, political ideology and historical experience, an area where the application of CDA may well in the future become an integral part of marketing strategy and therefore useful in communicating to specific stakeholders. The analysis of context has special emphasis in corporate visual texts as they need to identify the context within which signs are created and decoded. What influences caused the sign-maker to make a choice from a range of possibilities?

Making Corporate Pictures Talk

The process of corporate sign-making begins in the public affairs department, and proceeds through briefings to designers, photographers and other department heads, all of whom have different agendas. A dyadic process takes place within that corporate discourse. All that needs to be noted is that the sign-making team contains people who live within discourses that vary according to social class, education, political ideology and ethics. The semiotician Professor Thomas Sebeok (1991) uses a somewhat prolix statement to describe what emerges from such a multivariate team as 'an homology of spatiotemporal transition possibilities', which means in plain English: you pays your money but the end reader will still take away their own choice of meaning regardless of whether it is what the company intended or not. In semiotics meaning can be reduced to discrete items called syntagms. They may refer to one element of meaning in a logo or to a wider meaning transmitted by one part of a page, the whole page or the total brochure.

One of the criticisms of corporate brochures is that sign-makers fail to analyse each item of meaning and fail to assess the cumulative effect of those items on the page and how meaning changes page upon page, creating its own narrative with the whole coming together as one final, but possibly different meaning. Points can be identified where choices were made within the genre. The viewer, for example, takes hold of the brochure and it immediately speaks in terms of material signs. It may be glossy, on coated paper, A4 size, with a hard spine, but there were other choices that could have been made and those choices identify a decision made for some reason by the creator of the message in the first place.

It is important to identify such paradigm points where viewers will consciously or unconsciously ask themselves why that colour, why that size, why that model? With such an approach any analysis takes on a structure and with it a shift away from subjectivity. With iconic signs the signified element can create aberrant decoding in the sense that a religious icon such as a cross can signify different meanings to, say a Russian orthodox theologian compared to a Roman Catholic equivalent. Some icons are continually in a state of change. Sunglasses, for example, will offer a different meaning when displayed in the window of an optician to their presence in a photograph of a celebrity in the glossy British *Hello* magazine. The arbitrary relationship between signifier and signified is important because the arbitrary meaning is mediated by the social discourse within which different viewers move. Semiotic analysis helps describe and understand how people produce and communicate meaning in social settings. The level of theoretical knowledge carried by the managers in charge of the process makes them manage more effectively in terms of conveying a message to internal and external audiences within and without their stakeholder universe. The application of what were previously only academic concepts increases the efficiency of managers analysing the message around a product, a corporate message or indeed a stakeholder relationship. In making this application the manager needs to make a cognitive jump from the more normal application of academic semiotic theory to day-to-day business practice.

A Visual Language

What is written or what we might term visual language could be described as an 'action verb' which may be in pictures realised through shapes and elements that we term vectors. These may be realised by a finger pointing, an outstretched arm or the line of a building, roof or road. Pictorial design not only reproduces the structure of reality, it produces images of reality bound to social institutions within which the pictures are produced and read. They are ideological. When participants in a picture are shown to be doing something to each other they are connected by a vector, which creates its own narrative. This narrative can be used to show the participants in terms of ideology, class, and other generalised and less stable meanings which may or may not signify codes acceptable to the target viewer. Codes only work if the society within which they are used accepts them. In the case of brochures (and indeed film and video), vectors show an unfolding action page upon page. The actor is the participant from which the narrative or vector derives.

Where there are two participants in the visual proposition, one is the actor and one is the goal. The actor and goal thus compare to a transitive verb with the subject acting upon the object. The actor and the goal tend to be the most salient of the participants and the way they contrast with background, colour, and sharpness of focus or even as a psychological salience which emphasises elements in the meaning process.

A visual with one participant, staring at the camera, that is, at the viewer, is closer to intransitive verbs such as 'go forth' which has its own imperative, or demand (on the viewer). Kress and van Leeuwen (1996) suggest there are other invisible participants. They describe what they term the 'represented participant' who may be the subject of the communication and may be an abstract concept. They designate the viewer as a participant who plays different roles depending upon the positioning and attitudes of the other participants who may be staring straight to camera and thus making a 'demand' on the viewer, or staring off camera and using what if written could form an objective statement. In some cases the sign-maker may be a participant, establishing a strong sense of presence the viewer cannot ignore.

Participants may act together for one purpose and as such act as one participant. A tool becomes an extension of the actor, what is called a 'circumstance of means', and must be seen as part of the actor. In corporate visuals, for example, the pen in the hand or the mobile phone becomes a circumstance of means and adds to or adjusts the actor's meaning. The concept of vectoring, like grammar, forms a base for semiotic analysis.

How then do the participants fit together to make a larger statement? There is a reasonably low degree of modality because the background may be plain. The human participants are not the primary subject of the meaning process but the creators of the meaning through their concentration on other participants.

The vectoring leads the eye through framing which in the case of the primary vector, a human's arm, maybe a white shirt) against the black of the background. If the subject is a person and the second human is a customer and could therefore be referred to as the superordinate participant. At the viewer's first glance the superordinate participant is the first human who may be pointing, looking serious and carrying the authority of a clipboard and indeed a pen as an extension to his hand. The viewer as an implied participant receives no direct demand. The viewer has become an implied participant watching a discussion between two authoritative participants. A pen, if present, would be a 'circumstance of means' and in doing so takes an additional iconic authority.

Through advertising and other culture specific situations, executives around a table in discussion are frequently shown with a pen pointing at a document or flip chart to give emphasis. The first participant could be established as the 'given' and is an authority and thus in a power relationship. He would be seen as the representative of the company who knows about the product, concept or service.

The materiality modes chosen by the manager or sign-maker could include high gloss paper, full colour, hard-spine binding for a brochure for example, the paper size A4 and a variable use of type size. The degree of focus and say a dark background are all actors in the communication process and the manager who understands these many factors is the more efficient manager compared to their colleagues. To some extent some codes reinforce sensory allusions. The extra implied participant, the viewer, is in the sense of being a member of an elite group of represented participants. This is an implied abstract coding.

One Piece at a Time

The information item or primary informational subject, what is generally called a syntagm by social scientists, is usually placed centrally in most commercial items. The surrounding elements lend information and purpose to that subject who becomes both actor and goal. This creates a relay effect by passing additional information to any additional participant, not necessarily a human being who becomes the goal. Salience is generated through the placement of participants in such a way that they create their own framing. The context and socially identifiable articulations of any human participants, possibly in upper socioeconomic groups, will make a reference contextually to comfortable lifestyles, which can be enhanced through purchase of what the sign-maker sees as a metonymic symbol of 'good living'. The colour content is above the naturalistic in terms of saturation but in metalinguistic terms it could be normal within that context.

Is there, for example, ellipsis, that is, something left out but assumed? What has been left out is any reference to why that item is being identified without any statement of what it is or why it has been selected. There can be too great a visual ellipsis as a result. Is there any deviance? As a result of the cultural classification system there can be deviance on the part of the recipient who may refuse to be part of the community defined by the sign-producing paradigm. There can be deviance as a result of clothes and classical style of a human participant which could exclude customers who have high disposable incomes yet do not subscribe to a classical form of dress and posture. Indeed many in the world of the media, the arts and that of the entrepreneur might reject such icons yet still buy and market 'high-end objects'.

Effective communication requires participants to make their message maximally understandable in a particular context. That context may be a social structure marked by power differences which affect understanding. As Kress and van Leeuwen maintain (1996) we should note from where, socioculturally, the sign-maker(s) have chosen forms for the expression of what they have in mind, forms they see as most apt in the given context. There is a lacuna between data collected by social semiotic application and subjective criteria normally used by public affairs practitioners. The varying levels of training in visual comprehension differ markedly between executives from different global environments and education. These variations can be analysed with some accuracy through the creation and then application of social discourse analysis.

AIDA is in Charge

A classic AIDA business model of Attention, Interest, Desire, Action, seems to meet the need. It is concerned solely with the interaction between text and viewer and, as such, emphasises the extent to which the ideas of the sign-maker are most likely to be decoded. It could thus form a simple template for practitioners who have little training in semiotic theory. If the D and the A of AIDA are compressed into one as in corporate communications there is not necessarily a need for physical action as in the sales or marketing area. The action needed may well be a change of attitude and the psychological slide from desire to action, which itself may be abstract and require discrete research to differentiate. Pulling the threads together an AIDA template might look like this:

Attention

1.   identify participants, signifiers and signifieds, plus causal relationships;

2.   note linear narrative and vectoring;

3.   score colour classification;

4.   view perspective, locative circumstances leading to criterial factors;

Interest

5.   semiotic codes and social meaning;

Desire and **Action**

6.   salience of participants that encourage action;

7.   caption/text relationship;

8.   visual ellipsis;

9.   non-linear compositional factors;

10.   deviance.

This template with its ten ingredients provides the core data needed for everyday business practitioner use. In the case of the analysis of a front or back cover of a brochure, additional sub-sets of the questions are needed. This is because the front and back cover visuals perform the critical task of holding attention until the viewer examines the subsequent pages. Because of the quantity of many business communications and usually a shortage of time by target viewers to read it, visuals must speak as loudly as written words. If the visuals do not impart meaning at the attention stage the viewer will not even read the text.

What Have We Learnt?

What then have we learnt that is fresh from this analysis using semiotic concepts? It could be said that many of the factors would have been identified by any experienced communications practitioner. It could be argued, perhaps, that an approach where abstract concepts can be transformed into structured templates must help create consistency and, by doing so, improve the quality of meaning transfer in corporate terms. The process will thus help reduce the level of subjectivity, which currently dominates management decision making. As we consider the coming decade it is obvious that the manager's theoretical base must deepen. Talk of maintaining more complex communications as a response to the moral, political and stakeholder demands requires a psychological understanding of communications theory.

Social Semiotics and Discourse Analysis

Social semiotics is a branch of mainstream social science, an attempt to describe and understand how people produce and communicate meaning in specific social settings, whether they are discrete situations at home or with the family, or settings in which sign-making is well institutionalised and hemmed in by habits, conventions and rules. Social semiotics as sign-making in society is so varied an activity with so many psychological overtones that any attempt to capture it in general theory is likely to fail. It is necessary to consider the concept of 'discourse' and, in doing so, as mentioned earlier, explain how theories of discourse have been developed and conflated into CDA. This is relevant and applicable to the day-to-day practice of managers. It will help them disengage the hard factual data of 'what is there' in a picture (that is, a car, a driver, the countryside and so on) from the interpretation of that data. Hopefully it will help reduce the subjectivity caused by the communication analyst's own social and corporate cultural background.

Discourse analysis is defined in *The Icon Critical Dictionary of Postmodern Thought* (Simm, 1998) as: 'the study of the use of language as it flows or unfolds, as opposed to the rather atomistic sentencebased focus of stylists or traditional linguistics speakers who make sense of utterances because they are embedded within a hinterland of assumptions and expectations about what speech is and how it functions.' Every community shares a body of knowledge which is implicitly activated by any one semantic exchange. This body of knowledge shapes the norms of intelligibility, which will determine whether or not a statement is perceived as true, clear or relevant. Gunther Kress expands on this when he says:

> *Discourses are systematically organised sets of statements which give expression to the meanings and values of an institution. Beyond that, they define and delimit what it is possible to say and not possible to say with respect to the area of concern of that institution, whether marginally or centrally. A discourse provides a set of possible statements about a given area, and organises and gives structure to the manner in which a particular topic, object, process is to be talked about. In that it provides descriptions, rules, permissions and prohibitions of social and individual actions. (1985)*

Creating such sets of rules means that specialist fields, especially in the commercial world of marketing, sales promotion and public relations, will generate their own discourse and create a power dominance, which flows both ways during the sign-maker/viewer relationship. Writers such as Gee (1999) go further. Gee creates a distinction between discourse (lower case 'd,') which applies to linguistic discourse, and Discourse (upper case 'D') which includes all those factors such as the body, clothes, gestures, actions, interactions, symbols, values, attitudes, emotions which at the right place and at the right time constitute the intercommunication of continuous and developing meaning between humans within a discrete context. Gee argues (1999) that humans are particularly adept at melding all these linguistic and non-linguistic factors together, often with the result that we become members of a number of different discourses, which often themselves influence each other in positive and negative ways, producing what he calls their own 'hybrids'.

Gee sums it up by saying that Discourse (caps 'D') is the different way in which we humans integrate language and non-language 'stuff', such as different ways of thinking, acting, interacting, valuing, feeling, believing, and using symbols, tools and objects in the right places at the right times so as to enact and recognise different identities and activities, give the material world certain meanings, distribute social goods in a certain way, make certain meaningful connections in our experience, and privilege certain symbol systems and ways of knowing over others (Gee, 1999). It will be seen that this area of inclusion matches many of the elements described earlier that make up a corporate positioning in terms of its reputation and communication with the outside world. In this chapter the relevance of the concept of discourse (henceforth mean Discourse with an upper case 'D' whenever the word 'discourse', is mentioned with or without a caps 'D') to the theme of this work, especially when Gee comments:

> *Discourses are always embedded in a medley of social institutions, and often involve various 'props' like books and magazines of various sorts. In the end a Discourse is a 'dance' that exists in the abstract as a coordinated pattern of words, deeds, values, beliefs, symbols, tools, objects, times, and places and in the here and now as a performance that is recognisable as just such a coordination. Like a dance, the performance here and now is never exactly the same. (1999)*

In commercial literature there are fewer well-defined boundaries to discourse because new ones are constantly being created, old ones changed and boundaries forced outwards by professional communicators, especially in the field of advertising where there are attempts on a continuing basis to create new techniques for persuasion.

As Gee (1999) talks of the cultural models underlying discourse in general, making the point that they (the ingredients both conscious and unconscious) 'are usually not completely stored in any one person's head. Rather, they are distributed across the different sorts of "expertise" and viewpoints found in the group (Hutchins, 1995, Shore, 1996), much like a plot to a story (or pieces of a puzzle) that different people have different bits of and which they can potentially share in order to mutually develop the "big picture"'. This same configuration takes place within corporate discourse which also contains the socially based inputs discussed by Gee (1999) along with company ingredients that are frequently more tightly controlled because they are unidirectional and informed by senior management who maintain a power position over subordinates. In addition, the process is informed by the wider cohort of professional qualifications or interests within which the employees move, that is the world of accountancy, marketing, public affairs and other discrete skills maintained within a discourse which is based around the requirements of their membership of professional institutions. Gee likens the non-commercial discourse to a giant map with each Discourse represented on the map like a country but with movable boundaries that can slide around. The map can be placed on top of any language, action, or interaction the analyst is studying. The boundaries when moved around negotiate with others as reflections change. The map thus offers a way to understand what is seen in relation to a full set of Discourses in an institution or the society as a whole. Such a virtual map can be a Discourse grid against which thought, language, action and interaction are viewed. It would be of course an ever-changing map and will include, inter alia, some of the ingredients above such as the internal culture of an organisation, the shorter-term policies and views expressed through internal 'house magazines', seminars, conferences and departmental briefings which purport to represent the views of management. Of equal importance is the cohort effect, which frequently causes conflation from what is termed 'secondary opinion-forming groups' (Watts, 1970).

These groups of people, through their organisations, influence staff within a company because of the specialist training or qualifications they, the staff, receive or are receiving as members of discrete areas of specialisation. In some cases that influence is highly structured as in the case of accountants, lawyers and executives with business degrees. In some cases it is informal and takes place through seminars and short-term courses held in the local branches of professional bodies.

As a result of this, and pressures from within employee, social and domestic groups, there can be an extension even of Gee's concept of what are termed opinion-forming 'reference groups' (Watts 1970) that are overlooked by the analyst because, as the name implies, they describe those opinion-forming groups to which the manager 'refers' for the significant influences within their lives. As we discussed earlier in this book, the changes reported on the Millennial age group worldwide are altering many of these influence groups and the changes are becoming increasingly difficult to record and apply usable metrics. To apply discourse analysis to the visual, however, and in particular to the commercial visual, the assessment must be applied globally in any consideration of sociocultural influence and applied wider than the aesthetic rules normally applied to visual analysis. This means working towards what Kress and van Leeuwen call in the subtitle of their book (1996) a 'visual grammar'. This should not be an attempt to translate grammatical terms such as nouns, verbs, adverbs, phrases and so on into a visual format, although there will be times when such analogies can be usefully applied. The visual speaks with its own authority and with its own system that suggests how meaning is decoded. As the descriptive phrase 'critical discourse analysis' has been discussed it is necessary to define and explain its meaning in more detail within the context of this chapter and explain how it might inform practical methodologies in the future. The term 'critical discourse analysis' or CDA is used here to describe those analytical factors that can be grouped together as part of the sociocultural underpinning and power relationships which influence the way meaning is transferred (Gee, 1999). Such underpinnings are not only the social, cultural and power stimulus which go to make up a part of the discourse, but the relationships, their genesis of attitudes and cultural structures, the way they may or may not support the corporate cultural *status quo* and perhaps create their own changes or even cause adjustments to the boardroom policies passed down the management hierarchy for implementation (Hayes and Watts, 1986). There is the possibility always extant in commercial analysis that the products of the sign-maker can become sanitised as a result of inputs from managers senior to the sign-maker and whose views are regarded as sacrosanct. They are still, however, in the active form within which they have been created if the sign-maker is viewed in both a singular and plural form. During the process by which the sign-maker(s) 'manufacture' the final artefact, a number of paradigm choices within the genre take place. It is possible to classify the paradigmatic choices available to the sign-maker without attempting to identify the social semiotic process behind the choices. The classification may need to contain an element of subjectivity because without independent research based on interviews with those involved in the selection process it cannot be known what parameters were set by the senior managers who briefed the sign-maker, nor can it be identified what Hodge and Kress (1998) would call: 'Logonomic systems which constrain social behaviour through rules prescribing semiotic production; who is able/forbidden to produce or receive what meanings under what circumstances and in what codes.'

To function they must rely on known categories and rules and active enforcers with means of communication and enforcement (Hodge and Kress, 1998). Only those systems suitable for use in analysis of a finished product are considered here. That is the final visual text as an articulation of the company positioning strategy obtained by interview and in what form those meanings were transferred by means of artefacts such as reports, brochures or promotions. Any model created must draw upon CDA and include a checklist of tools of enquiry, which forms a basis for cross-checking results. In preparing the following section on the subject of critical discourse, we have drawn upon the seminal work of Barker and Galasinski (2001). Barker and Galasinski argue that within CDA 'analyses are interpretative: they are laden with researchers' views and beliefs'.

They maintain that 'if the linguistic analysis is anchored within systemicfunctional linguistics it can help reduce the interpretative aspect of analysing by anchoring it on the discourse form itself'. By using a template approach a framework could be created within which managers can carry out their analysis and the subjective interpretative element reduced.

Historicity and the Visual Lexis

Discourse analysis is not a 'snapshot' of social and cultural interactions, which are taking place during one moment in time. There is a historicity present by which the images in visual communication refer to, or are the product of, earlier images which themselves grew from their antecedents. The area of corporate identity is a cauldron of such intertextuality where art, applied design and corporate logo systems feed off each other to produce what Fairclough (1989) calls their own 'order of discourse'. The paradigmatic process informs understanding of the influences on the sign-maker as part of the CDA that can be used to consider the vocabulary or lexis of items used by the sign-maker. There is a need to itemise visual ingredients as signifiers without context, even assuming their signifieds may change when considered within context. In comparison with other pages within a brochure or in comparison with similar brochures produced at another time, the mere comparison of the visual vocabulary transfers its own meaning.

The Objectives of the Above Analysis

What then has been the business objective of this part of the chapter?

The answer is that the questioning process identifies and then separates two functions: at one level it provides an approach to the identification of factual data in a business visual text focusing on what is there and about which there should be little debate, it might, for example, list a picture as containing a car, a tree and a driver. These are hard facts only. At a second level a template can also operate on those areas where the subjectivity of the analyst is likely to intrude into the interpretation.

It is then that CDA helps reduce the subjectivity of the interpretation. The analyst will bring to each project an ethnic, a social and indeed a corporate cultural background. The more these elements are reduced in influence as part of the interpretative process the more likely it is the business leader and practitioner will arrive at solutions that align with colleagues who too could use these techniques. Together they will achieve a greater understanding of the visual texts.

The elements discussed form a foundation upon which the reader could develop a selection of concepts into a format from which practical tools could be created. Business academics can embrace these tasks and work to have them available as a normal element within their daily practice assuming they are senior managers. With such tools practitioners will be able to compete in what will become a more competitive environment in the years ahead.

At the beginning of the chapter, business training was discussed in the shape of MBAs, and the new Master's degree in Management aimed at graduates before they start work. From there the argument moved forward through an opening door which gave access to a significant range of opportunities such as MOOC university links and professional bodies seeking university accreditation for existing qualifications.

The final part of the chapter emphasised the potential of untended academic grasslands which though accepted as important by non-business academics has seldom been ploughed by trainers searching for new skills to improve management practice. The going was sometimes difficult but, as with all new ideas, progress needed concentrated effort and a determination to reach and acquire new skills. In the chapter we have considered the methodologies in some depth that will be needed for the projection of corporate reputations into the new evolving global market place.

In the next chapter we draw strings together and consider two concerns for the decade ahead. What message will become pre-eminent regarding corporate communications strategy and the methodologies needed to project those strategies?

Summary

1.   In the coming decade business leaders need to be multi-skilled and capable of drawing upon and assimilating academic disciplines seldom considered as appropriate for business application. Many of the skills are seen as of academic relevance and frequently have not been viewed as having obvious management application. In fact as we show they do have relevance.

2.   Business training is expanding in terms of syllabus content and provision of new training opportunities for every level of management both at Board level and at middle management.

3.   Leaders must become lifetime students; always learning and always exploring new disciplines that could help them establish global perspectives.

Chapter 8

The Ties that Bind: Networking Smart for Shared Value

Networking is at the heart of an emerging focus on soft assets – reputation and trust centred on people and authentic communication. Along with navigating the global environment, negotiating win–win solutions and reframing narratives from a stakeholder perspective, networking is a critical skill for leaders. This is underlined by recent research in the public diplomacy literature (Hayes, 2012). Few leaders, however, feel at ease outside their comfort zone, networking with a whole new ecosystem of stakeholders. Networking needs to be undertaken proactively, coherently and systematically. It has always been the age of the networker; it's just that it has taken on a life of its own thanks to marketing and headhunting.

The network is the signature form of organisation in the information age, just as bureaucracy stamped the industrial age, hierarchy controlled the agrarian one and the small group roamed in the nomadic era (as various books on the subject describe social evolution). This has obviously had implications for the global system with networks at the heart of the new global economy. Power is shifting towards those with authority based on knowledge and certain psychological/political skills. What is needed is more co-creation, replacing hierarchical institutions with lateral networking, outsiders belonging to the internal network. This requires collaboration and a stakeholder orientation.

Networking in Networks

E.M. Forster, the English novelist brought up partly in India, was surely prescient in writing: 'Live in fragments no longer. Only connect.' He wrote the novel *Howard's End* in 1910 before networking became a popular term among career advisers and self-help gurus, let alone C-Suite advisers much later in the twentieth century. He was writing at a time when foreign travel was an adventure limited to the wealthy few and of course well before the Internet led to the virtual global network.

The well-known sociologist of the information age, Manuel Castells, described it well in his book *The New Public Sphere* (2008): 'A network based social structure is a highly dynamic, open system, susceptible to innovating without threatening its balance.' More prosaically, a true network works because so much social capital has been expanded on it.

Ironically it is networking in this new networks era that will lead to a much more effective stakeholder approach, because corporations, governments and civil society organisations as much as individuals are needing to collaborate as well as compete, sharing information as much as other resources, and by so doing are adding value to the overall system, whether team, organisation, city, nation or global environment. All these elements need to be addressed in a coordinated way not viewed as distinct or separate entities. Professor Bruce Cronin (2014) (Greenwich University Business School, UK), a leader in social network analysis, argues that the strength of stakeholder relations can be measured and that key influencers can be identified. The Tomorrow's Company Report (2014) highlights four key aspects to creating efficient relationships (with stakeholders), namely identifying, tuning in, measuring and reporting the efficiency of them. For example, we have referred to the fact that public policy and business school topics are rarely integrated. Yet government is integral to finance and marketing, just as the business mind-set could do with being brought into the public policy process more. Moreover, the future will see alternative ideas emerging from other cultures. In the UK there exists the legal contract-based nature of all business activity. In many other parts of the world it is common to have commercial relations based more on family ties, underpinned by trust. Western B-School courses mainly assume a Western economic model. In China, despite some 'reforms', the government is the prime market regulator and some traditional models of capitalism do not exist.

Talking of China, given the absence of reliable information on city pollution in the past, networking via micro blogging among (a new form of) NGOs, schools, parents and children has forced the Government to 'come clean' about the need to find a better balance between economic growth and environmental pollution contributing to ill-health. As a popular Chinese saying has it: 'While truth is still tying its shoelaces, rumour has already run a whole lap around China.'

Earlier in the book we talked about the growth of cities on our thinking and in particular how we network at that level. Nigeria is arguably the worst run of the world's seven most populated cities, yet its largest city Lagos seems to have turned a corner in governance. Despite inequalities and exploding population (21,000,000), government, business and civil society are collaborating to upgrade the city. This is due to devolving power to cities from corrupt and over-centralised national government, which is too remote. Local elections have forced candidates to demonstrate pragmatism and competence. They also understand that if they build better roads, the more business and citizens will pay in service charges and taxes, creating a virtuous circle. In an ethnically and religiously diverse metropolis, politicians cannot afford to pit one group against another. Also, when their neighbourhoods are affected, the growing middle class is more likely to insist on better governance. Cities can help some countries. Nigeria is close to becoming the largest economy in Africa to the consternation of South Africa.

Strategic and Systematic Approach

Networks are structures, albeit dynamic ones, but networking is a process much in need of a strategic and systematic approach. Needless to say each of us participates in small groups most of the time, adding shared value in incremental ways. With each new set of connections, we are probably not conscious how connected things really are. We've all heard about 'Six degrees of separation', which by now is probably half that as a result of social media. (This topic by the way deserves at least another chapter, if not another book.) Networking gurus talk of the strength of 'weak ties', due to the 'novelty of information' being provided by the person someone in your close network knows, but you don't!

Social Capital

The key word here is 'social'. Economics has evolved to be quite individualistic, the extent depending on different capitalist models. Politics is generally communitarian operating at a national level, yet at a global level often conflicting. But the key to networking in an interdependent and interconnected world is social capital. This term first came into public consciousness in Robert Putnam's seminal book *Bowling Alone* (2000) which charted the decline of 'social connectedness' in American communities, leading to a greater sense of civic community. The authors cite the richly networked societies hundreds of years ago in the city–states of Northern Italy, based on these criteria, leading to an intellectual and cultural Renaissance. These have their parallels today in the dense clusters of Silicon Valley and examples in other parts of the world, where boundaries are porous and communities expand via co-creation. Social capital now is a balance of global/local, looking outside and in simultaneously, with self-assertive individuality joined at the hip with others. The key to social life is not unfettered competition, nor universal cooperation, but a subtle mix of the two – competing fiercely to join up with the most attractive cooperators. For companies it is the stakeholder concept that is a mutually reinforcing way, not just to differentiate itself competitively but also to play a broader role in human life. It is a new equilibrium between governments, business and civil society in which individuals and organisations become more involved in their communities whether at local, national or global level.

Cultural Dimension

It is significant in the context of this book's theme that business leaders and their managers tend to have a fix on the economics, needless to say, and possibly the politics, although even that is sometimes outside 'the comfort zone'. Yet they tend to be inept when it comes to society and its cultural overtones. In the global world, while cultures are not susceptible to homogenisation, networking embraces both the Asian emphasis on community and the Western one on 'us and them'. This perhaps can lead to a greater fusion, thus added value. But managers need what is called 'global dexterity' to not only diagnose cultural differences, but adjust behaviour in a culturally distinct setting. A Chinese MBA student going to a networking event in the US is aware of American styles of assertiveness and self-promotion, yet it goes against the notions of power and respect ingrained in him since childhood. According to a book on this topic, business school 'immersion' trips are a good start, but it does not equip people to become effective global leaders. Globalisation and the Internet have changed the way we do things, having a profound effect on the concept of networking.

Glue and Grease

We should try and evoke the spirit of Verona and Venice going forward. It is also to be hoped that there may a resurgence of interest in 'systems theory', both for its scientific approach to management and its human touch. So there is a lot riding on the concepts of networks and networking to build the glue (purpose) with the grease (trust). This explosion of lateral connections in a variety of contexts and linkages will be successful the more social capital they contain, perhaps leading to a greater reservoir of trust and bountiful behaviour.

This leads on to definitions. This author (RH) has always considered himself a relatively active networker, and certainly is known as one. He has always admired others with amazing networks that are put to good use – which are namely scalable. The Chinese and Indian 'diaspora' are good examples of dense networks. The overseas Chinese are a network of networkers. 'Guanxi' or connections is the chief reason given for the success of the more than 50,000,000 ethnic Chinese people worldwide. Though by no means a homogeneous group, they have largely thrived by developing a business structure based on entrepreneurial, family-owned firms that operate easily with one another across borders and between institutions. Their business methods are aimed at establishing trust as well as lowering transaction costs. The Chinese diaspora are the biggest foreign investors in China, investing more than the US, Japan and the EU combined, mainly moving into the booming South East coastal provinces, from where most originate. Some are also buying up properties and businesses in London! The importance of clan and language will gradually lose force; time no doubt for this group to adapt again. Another competitive edge of the overseas Chinese has always been adaptability, an important characteristic of networking. Control of networking is passing to a new generation with new forms springing up as old 'Guanxi' ties loosen. These are alumni of US business schools, as many of the next generation are now being educated internationally. The same is true of the Indian diaspora, which is very strong in places such as the UK, the US and elsewhere. One interesting example is the case of Gujaratis in the US. By the 1970s, they had distinguished themselves from other Indian groups by entering small businesses and becoming employers themselves. The largest sub-group, known as Patels, famously entered the hotel industry in America, purchasing motels that were going out of business as oil prices rose and road travel fell. They achieved this by relying on interest-free loans from friends and family. They are considered one of the most successful and affluent of the South Asian settlers.

From Nations to Networks

The world is moving from a collection of nation states to a collection of networks. Information offers choice; choice motivates interaction; and peoples' interactions form the network of society. Francis Fukuyama (1995) wrote that high levels of trust in Asian societies explains the relative stability and success of much of this part of the world, because 'they put trust at the centre of a web of relationships'. High-trust societies foster encouragement and moral pressure in addition to material incentives. Just as in traditional Italian cities, economic success and social cohesion can arise from community reinforcement, based around shared values via networks. In some of these emerging markets more women are coming to prominence as CEOs. This means more networking and a new attitude to career management, particularly as with ageing populations, there are more senior, highly experienced freelancers able to contribute. Whereas continuous learning and networking is a challenge, we all have a chance to shape our work to suit our lives as well as add societal value, whether at a local, national or global level – or all three. The term 'portfolio life' was coined by British management guru Charles Handy and combines free work, charity work, study and paid work which not only contributes to personal fulfilment, but can add value to organisations, build coalitions and fuel consulting resources in the form of informal networks. These 'netweavers', as they are called, facilitate and curate, act as strategic brokers, pulling together the right people, act creatively, ensuring the job gets done.

Collaboration in business is no longer confined to conventional two-company alliances. Today, groups of companies are linking themselves together often for a common purpose leading to a new form of cooperation. These clusters join together in an overlapping relationship, with collective governance ensuring that a network is more than a haphazard collection of alliances.

Enlightened Serendipity

Tom Peters, management writer and co-author of the seminal business book *In Search Of Excellence* (Peters and Waterman, 1982) rightly made the point that: 'Your power is always directly proportional to the thickness of your rolodex and the time you spend maintaining it.' In this author's (RH) experience you need to follow-up or fail, stay in touch regularly and maintain the quality of contacts. Nicholas Taleb, author of *Black Swan* (2007), about the randomness of the financial markets recommended: 'maximising the serendipity around you'. This author (RH) has regularly described it as: 'Enlightened Serendipity, an investment not a transaction, an attitude to life, as much as about marketing, targeting, a process, all leading to collaborative exchange.'

One of the paradoxes of networking is the strength of weak ties. Namely how connections at the edge of peoples' networks, rather than at the core, boost innovation by dint of building bridges as the network expands across the boundaries of social groups.

The Law of 10

The law of 10 in networking, leaving aside American 'auteur' Woody Allen's famous dictum that '90 per cent of life is showing up' is:

1. Small things count.
2. Quality not quantity of contacts.
3. Long-term relationships based on trust.
4. Repeated interactions.
5. Thinking ahead – building goodwill early.
6. Seeking out informal settings.
7. Most useful contacts are weak connections.
8. Broad and deep – six degrees of separation.
9. Integrated system/broader lifestyle.
10. Way of behaving/stream of consciousness.

Systematic and Strategic

It is really an alignment of *issues*, the why, *information*, the what, *interfaces*, the who, with *influence* being the confluence of all three to adopt a win–win approach. Issues in this context means ascertaining the objectives, (areas of interest, subject areas and value system,) information (the knowledge, experience, contacts and expertise), the interface (targeting by research, data basing) and influence (power to decide, referrals, reputation, credibility and ultimately shaping the future). Essentially a networking programme divides into four key activities – *audit*, *target*, *promote* and *cultivate*. While successful, sustainable networking is largely a product of a proactive management approach, born of a vision and values supported by a tool-kit.

The *audit* is about finding out how you are currently perceived versus how you wish to be and plan a campaign to narrow the gap. Plot your immediate spheres of influence and connections, in turn plotting their spheres of influence and connections. Identify the barriers to wider influence and work out how to remove or at least overcome them. The 80/20 rule comes in here. Plan a programme of reaching a wider circle, infiltrating wheels within wheels. Remember you have to be a member of a group to influence another.

Target who/what should be your network and why. Research their agendas and interests. Identify their circle of contacts and connections. Inform yourself about what is going on and who is doing it. When you're off to a gathering for the first time, even up the odds by knowing as much as you can about what goes on and who goes. When you get there study the delegates list during the speeches! (Not everyone gets to go to the networking of networking events – The World Economic Forum at Davos and its regional versions – even there you will find networks within networks.)

Next *promote*. This means networking yourself or your organisation through events, receptions, joining suitable partnership and membership organisations. Publish results, achievements and circulate them to chosen targets. Empower yourself by mixing among the decision makers. Campaign with the media. This is enhanced now with new media. Many CEOs and senior managers we know are not good networkers, although there are some amazing exceptions. The question now is how do you network globally and use new media wisely, given the down as well as the upsides?

This leads on to *cultivate*. It is important to make good use of networking notables or third-party advocates. It is significant that academics and NGOs are usually more trusted than CEOs, always depending on the context. This is why partnerships between business, government, civil society, including universities and other groups are so important. You have to keep at it, contacting your key quality contacts at least five times a year according to professors of relationship marketing.

Above all the issues must be clear, the information parameters set and the interfaces listed by category and annotated with their interconnectedness. Then your and your organisation's network will becomes advocates working on your behalf. Only then can you truly achieve influence. Networks work best for you when you are resting and playing, because the hard graft has been done systematically and the investment in this strategic discipline made.

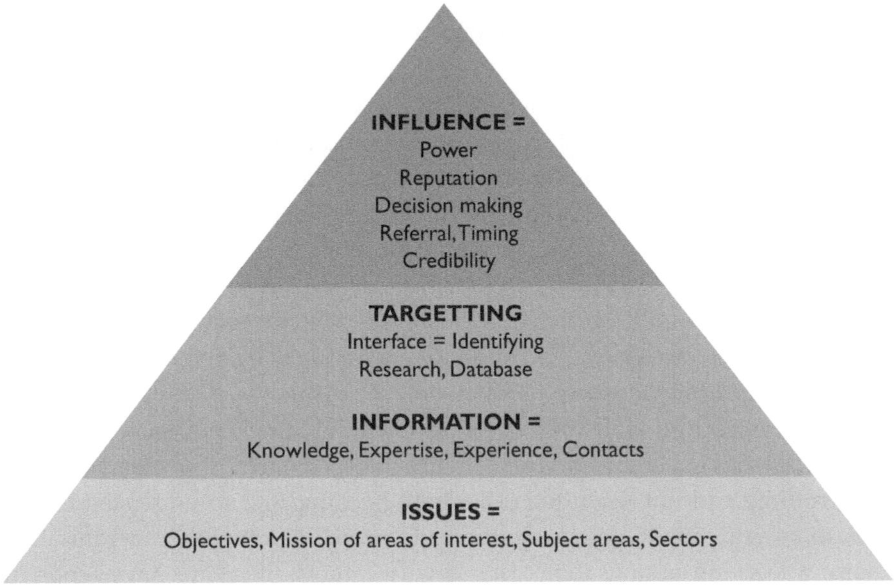

INFLUENCE =
Power
Reputation
Decision making
Referral, Timing
Credibility

TARGETTING
Interface = Identifying
Research, Database

INFORMATION =
Knowledge, Expertise, Experience, Contacts

ISSUES =
Objectives, Mission of areas of interest, Subject areas, Sectors

Figure 8.1   Matrix methodology
Source: Hayes, 1997.

Questions

1.   Who are the internal and external stakeholders?

2.   What and where are the networks of information?

3.   What is the cultural context greasing networks?

4.   With what organisations should you collaborate?

5.   Are you ready for appropriate thought-leadership?

New Technology of Social Relations

While successful, sustainable networking is largely a product of a proactive approach, born of vision and values, mission and culture, and there is clearly a methodology that is a combination of art and science. This new technology of social relations can have productive outcomes, not just for the individual or specific organisation, but also for groups of individuals and whole communities, local and global. Key elements are *listening, learning, linking* and *leading*. This involves 'sweat equity' because information is the currency. A wide-ranging network is therefore a sure way to become a 'thought leader', especially now when it is important to have a point of view, be distinctive. On the other hand, diplomats refer to a skill they need of 'deep listening', not something this author (RH) has experienced as a talent of senior managers. They tend to speak half the time and not listen the other half! Seeking first to understand, only then to be understood should be the watchword. A networked organisation is also a learning organisation. This is very important, as we have reported when companies can learn from local communities and NGOs, enabling them to improve their innovation, creativity and economic success.

Adding Value across the Network: A New Mind-set

Business leaders, often 'super connectors' themselves, are the nodes in a whole variety of networks involving key corporate and broader stakeholders. It is important to add value across the network – the concept of 'your story is now their story', as opposed to 'what's in it for me?' Networking really amounts to building bridges and crossing boundaries that unlock the patterns of the past or trap us in outmoded models of thinking and doing. 'It's thinking ahead, involving skilful analysis of the context, combined with astute networking and relationship building' (Kraus, 2006).

In summary, networking is at the heart of an emerging focus on soft assets – reputation and relationships, dialogue and diplomacy. The philosophy of networking is win–win, not win–lose as in the excesses of capitalism witnessed in recent years. We need a new equilibrium between individual rights and civic community, which networking is well placed to reconcile. Networking in a mutually reinforcing way, not just to keep the wolf from the door but also to lead and achieve personal growth is consistent with the stakeholder concept of business. It's a long-term contract, consistent with this book's approach to sustainable capitalism and governance. Networking works alongside navigating the complex environment, creating compelling narratives and negotiating win–win solutions to stakeholder dialogue. Despite the time and financial investment a systematic approach to networking demands, it can pay dividends. After all it is a mind-set that helps 'join the dots'.

Marcel Proust (1922) wrote: 'The real art of discovery consists not in finding new lands, but in seeing with new eyes.'

Summary

1.   Networking is an integral part of business leadership complementing navigation, negotiation and narrative development.

2.   Networking is as much a philosophy as a process, needing to be strategic and systematic, concentrating on weak as much as strong ties.

3.   Build equity in the social capital bank before you need it. It is a long-term investment.

The Past is Prologue

Former UN Secretary–General Kofi Anan remarked that 'globalisation of the economy implies globalisation of responsibility'. Kofi Anan was commenting on the need for connections between countries and institutions, the need for business, governments and civil society to collaborate.

In a recent speech, 'The Business of Changing the World' (2013), a former senior Gates Foundation representative, Kate James, argued that social media is an opportunity for social good, making connections and fostering collaboration at macro and micro levels on development issues. It's a question of social push–leadership pull. Water, for example, is key to energy, food, security, health and education, yet as water scarcity becomes all too real, complexity sets in and collaboration between many stakeholders becomes essential. Now conversations are possible between a whole new ecosystem of stakeholders via lateral networks operating in global and local communities. James argued that when she worked for Standard Chartered Bank, 10 per cent of employees in Kenya were either suffering from HIV/AIDS or looking after someone who was and therefore, 'the morally right thing to do is also the right thing to do for your business'.

Responsible Leadership

Certainly this whole approach requires alignment between corporate vision and values. This means a longer-term approach, support from the whole company and a resilient senior management team. It is predicated on responsible leadership, adjusting the corporate character and culture, the narrative being determined not just by market signals, but societal needs and the emergent expectations of stakeholders. These are linked to meaning and purpose, rather than simply material fulfilment. It is worrying that in this whole area of reputation and relationships, all intangible assets, many corporations face a mismatch between requirements and capabilities, woefully inadequate systems and strategies, let alone skills.

Smart Philanthropy

CSR efforts need to align with the bottom line, that interconnection between people, profit and planet. By facilitating market access, consumer engagement and employee motivation you begin to see a return on investment. This is particularly true in the emerging world where markets and social change interact. We are now living in a world of smart philanthropy, where the private sector works closely with governments at all levels and NGOs to co-create value via the network chain.

A New Face for Capitalism

As stressed during the book, we are not advocating the abolition of capitalism, rather its reform and greater involvement in solving macro issues. These are issues such as climate change and inequalities, along with micro issues in specific communities. It is significant that too few development charities have a good word to say about those corporations that set up in emerging countries in search of profit-making opportunities. Yet it's the investment they bring, the infrastructure they build, the technology they seed, the small firms they contract, not to mention the taxes they pay, that are doing more than anything to transform continents such as Africa, especially in the urban areas.

We must keep corporate responsibility and stakeholder engagement in perspective, always trying to align this with the core aim of capitalism. At a time of 'connected capitalism' it is unlikely that much will be achieved by corporate citizenship alone in overcoming global poverty, inequality and environmental pollution. It will not happen until this debate evolves to the point where global governance frameworks are put in place. Frameworks that effectively secure 'civil market behaviour' underpinning sustainable development, as espoused in *The Civil Corporation* (Zadek, 2004). Fortunately there is greater collaboration. In South Africa, President Mandela asked Mervyn King to write the King Report (2009) advocating the need for that country, after apartheid, to adopt a more inclusive governance approach, one that would focus on the need for corporate reporting to reflect the social impact of business. Some years later, Professor King is now chair of The International Integrated Reporting Council (IIRC), which is attempting to codify global reporting.

Stakeholder Strategies

It would be helpful, however, if company directors spent more time on stakeholder strategies and ethics, rather than purely the next quarterly earnings, even while accepting it is a delicate balancing act. However much one tries to put broader issues on the boardroom agenda, in our experience they tend to be drowned out by the tyranny of numbers – the urgent being confused with the important. In her report on levels of trust post financial crisis, Professor Hope-Hailey of Bath University, UK, found that some companies increased trust among employees resulting from the way they led in uncertain times (Corporate Research Forum, 2013). This meant 'walking the talk', not overpromising and especially communicating authentically. Amidst the various reports on the financial crisis, corporate scandals and managerial misconduct, a common denominator is in attributing the failures to the challenges of globalisation. There have been attempts to find a connection between corporate responsibility and transformational leadership of the kind shown by Nelson Mandela, grounded in morality, an understanding of leaders as servants in the Gandhi tradition. This is similar to authentic leadership, which theorists believe to be a root construct in the study of leadership linked to trust. It is significant though that NGOs remain more trusted than corporations. According to The Edelman Trust Barometer (2013), CEOs make the least credible spokespeople. This is a concern if it is accepted that CEOs should be playing a broader leadership role.

The Leadership Challenge

The problem with different leadership typologies is that they do not seem to adequately encompass the causes and implications of present leadership challenges, rooted in the shareholder versus stakeholder implications of globalisation and Internet connectivity. At a time of deep distrust of leaders and institutions, this is worrying. Present leaders remain focused on micro-level, internal organisation perspectives. Yet only by bridging the organisational and individual level of corporate responsibility does one do justice to the complexity of issues and collaboration tasks current leaders must address. Sadly it is not in the comfort zone nor skills base of most senior management, even if there are some marvellous exceptions.

Responsible leadership is an emerging concept at the overlap of studies in leadership, ethics, strategic communications and public diplomacy. The concept attempts to answer the question: who is responsible for what and to whom in an interconnected and interdependent world? We have tried to examine this through a variety of prisms in this book. So protecting human rights, enforcing labour standards, fighting corruption and saving the natural habitat remain largely unaddressed, certainly not in a coherent way. Responsible leaders can gradually change the ethical culture of an organisation over time via deliberative practice and discursive conflict resolution, balancing competing interests. Yet the external governance issues still need to be resolved.

Finding a True Voice

A combination of globalisation, with its lack of shared values, governance gaps as well as shining a spotlight on bad behaviour is exerting pressure on companies to build their moral legitimacy and maintain trusted relationships. This at least has the benefit of leveraging social capital. Given leadership must be authentic, this begins with 'the communicative organisation' (as defined by the Global Alliance for Public Relations (2012) which is also cooperating with the IIRC). Authentic leaders have conviction, meaning they need to connect to that part of the bigger picture they can influence. This is achieved by digging deep into experience and character, listening and finding a true voice. It means engaging in dialogue and adopting a more diplomatic approach. This should have an impact on ethical corporate culture. In a fast-changing and uncertain world of 24/7 media scrutiny, stakeholders seek meaning from their leaders, not merely performance indicators, profits, but also purpose. An authentic leader anticipates the future, wishes to create part of it, commits to action and encourages others to follow. It is a pity that when global integration is a priority for many organisations and directly impacts human sustainability, with companies needing to deal with various societal cultures, this element is often missed. This is due to the obsession with economics and politics. Unfortunately there are far more questions than answers regarding culturally contingent aspects. But above all, what is required is clear vision underpinned by values.

A Multi-dimensional Mindset

So globalisation, the war for talent, digital communications, societal changes, the changing shape of organisations and aspirations of the next generation are all challenging twenty-first century leaders in new ways. The quest for more sustainable and ethical organisations brought on by scandals and scarcity has put enormous pressure on institutions and their leaders to perform against far wider criteria than simply successful commercial or policy performance.

Business leaders are certainly caught between a rock and a hard place, but where will these ambidexterous skills and mind-sets derive? Vision these days is no longer static or restricted to the board room Rather it is more about co-creation, sharing the future and tapping into all available networks to continually create new knowledge and add value. What is needed on the part of CEOs is a multidimensional mind-set. This comprises whole brain thinking, embracing the scientific and spiritual, emotional and rational, social, economic and political.

Redefining Business Purpose

Thus, as Professors Porter and Kramer (2011) said, there is no fixed trade-off between economy and environment. Firms should do both, which in turn promotes innovation. With capitalism under siege, diminished trust and politicians regulating, the purpose of business must be redefined. As they put it, value needs to be shared.

Governments and NGOs are partly to blame, by attempting to trade-off economic efficiency and social programmes. But it is our contention that the private sector must take a lead in linking economic with social value. This requires leaders to develop new skills and knowledge around collaboration, productivity and social need. Stakeholders are demanding that the corporate story should now be their story.

Governments/NGOs Learn New Ways

Business needs to step up to the plate and the moment for reconceptualising capitalism is now. Luckily social entrepreneurs are often well ahead of established corporations in discovering these opportunities, because they are not locked into narrow, traditional business thinking. Governments and NGOs also need to learn new ways. Given the greater collaboration needed between corporations, governments and civil society, a constraint is that few managers understand environmental and social issues. Just as few NGOs understand commercial issues. The same is true of business and political cross-over. This has implications for business school curricula and reframing the debate around environment, economics and ethics.

A Code of Business Ethics

Having a code of business ethics is also a hallmark of a well-managed company. The UK Institute of Business Ethics argues there is a growing demand for businesses not only to say they are ethical, but to prove they have ethical values embedded throughout their organisation and others in the supply chain network.

In the early 1980s people joked that an MBA course in ethics would be the shortest course in the curriculum. But now questions of trust and transparency have moved to the top of the political and business agenda, reflected in some MBA courses. In the twentieth century, jurists in the US and Europe gradually came to accept the idea that companies are institutions quite distinct from the collective interests of shareholders. So began the stakeholder idea more fully developed by R.E. Freeman.

For years there have been ethics officers, codes of conduct and whistle-blower facilities, but cultures tended to tolerate and sometimes reward unethical behaviour. As David Vogel of Haas Business School in the US put it: 'Culture always trumps compliance' (2008). There needs to be shared and inclusive values, clearly defined and communicated, inclusive relationships and inclusive reporting. Mark Goyder of Tomorrow's Company described it in 2003 like this: 'A future for business, which makes equal sense to staff, shareholders and society.'

A Long-term Business Focus

McKinsey (Barton, 2013) has launched a thought-leadership project to 'expand' the thinking of Boards beyond their more traditional emphasis on risk and compliance, to focus more on long-term, sustainable growth. Now that really would be helpful for furthering the stakeholder approach if this becomes a central narrative in boardrooms and policy chambers. But this will require a very open debate among governments, business, the financial community and civil society to move beyond a purely shareholder perspective. It will require more sophisticated communications approaches, embedding this thinking into the culture of organisations. Above all we need greater leadership, at institutional level, city level, national level and globally. Big data will either be a help or a hindrance.

Emerging expectations, massive changes, greater stakeholder empowerment and an ambiguous environment will require not only greater resilience on the part of leaders and the organisations they represent, but 'a BIG understanding'.

Anticipating the Future

There is a true involvement imperative for CEOs – to exert leadership on the public stage, forging relationships with multiple, interdependent stakeholders. The narrow approach on the demands of the financial community is no longer viable given today's complexity. The task of the CEO and other heads of organisations is to reframe the narrative, raising the bar higher, anticipating the future and creating it in a new spirit. As our former colleague and inspiration for this book, Millicent Danker (2011) wrote: 'The modern corporation is now expected to lead more and more for stakeholder value.' We remain optimistic, if impatient.

Bibliography and Recommended Reading[1]

Andriof, J., Waddock, S., Husted, B. and Sutherland Rahnan, S. (2002/3). *Unfolding Stakeholder Thinking*, Greenleaf.

APCO Worldwide (2008). Viewpoint, www.apcoworldwide.com.

Avolio, B. and Gardner, B. (2005). Authentic Leadership Development: Getting to the Root of Positive Forms of Leadership, *The Leadership Quarterly*, Elsevier.

Barker, B. (2013). *If Mayors Ruled the World, Dysfunctional Nations Rising Cities*, Yale University Press.

Barker, C. and Galasinski, D. (2001). *Cultural Studies and Discourse Analysis: A Dialogue on Language and Identity*, Sage Publications.

Barthes, R. (1982). *Image Music Text*, Flamingo.

Barthes, R. (1993). *Camera Lucida*, Flamingo.

Barton, D. (2013). 'Focusing on the Long Term', http://www.marketwired.com/press-release/cpp-investment-board-mckinsey-company-global-survey-signals-short-term-pressures-on-1793872.htm.

Bennis, W. (2003). *On Becoming a Leader*, Perseus.

Bishop, M. and Green, M. (2010). *The Road from Ruin*, Crown Business.

Bishop, M. and Green, M. (2014). *Philanthrocapitalism: How the Rich Can Save The World*, Crown Business.

---

1   All web sources were accessed during 2013 and 2014.

Brunswick Insight, (2013). The Future of Stakeholder Engagement, www. brunswickgroup.com.

Burchell, J. and Cook, J. (2006). Assessing the Impact of Stakeholder Dialogue, *Journal of Public Affairs*, 6, 210–27.

Canton, J. (2006). *The Extreme Future*, Institute for the Global Future.

Castells, M. (2008). The New Public Sphere: Global Civil Society, Communication Networks and Global Governance. *The Annals of the American Academy of Politics and Social Science*, 616, March, 78–93.

Charan, R., Carey, D. and Useen, M. (2013). *Boards That Lead: When To Take Charge, When To Partner and When To Stay Out of the Way*, Harvard Business Review Press.

Collins, J. (2001). *Good to Great*, Random House Business.

Corporate Research Forum. (2013). Trust Report, University of Bath, www. bath.ac.management/faculty.com.

Coulthard, M. (1985). *An Introduction to Discourse Analysis*, Longman.

Cronin. B. (2014). Speech to Strategic Communications Summit, University of Greenwich, UK, September.

Danker, M. (2011). Doctoral Research/Global Governance, Henley Business School/University of Reading.

Danker, M. (2012). Malaysia Lectures, Henley Business School/University of Reading.

de Saussure, F. (1966). *Course in General Linguistics*, edited by Charles Bally and Albert Sechehaye, translated by Wade Baskin, McGraw-Hill Book Company.

Das, G. (2002) *India Unbound*, Penguin.

Downing, S. (2008/9). Leading for Sustainability, White Paper Series, Henley Business School, www. henley.com.

Eco, U. (1984). *Semiotics and the Philosophy of Language*, Indiana University Press.

Edelman Worldwide. (2013). Edelman Trust Barometer, www.edelman.com/trust.

Elkington, J. (1997). *Cannibals with Forks: The Triple Bottom-Line of 21st Century Business*, Capstone.

Ericsson. (2013). 2020 – Shaping Ideas, http://global-influences.com/social/communication-nation/2020-shaping-ideas/.

EUROSME Conference. (2013). http://eurosme2013.eu/wp-content/uploads/2013/06/KJAER-GLOBAL_SME-2030.pdf.

Fairclough, N. (1989). *Language and Power*, Longman.

FCA. (2013). Financial Services Regulation and Enforcement: Recent Developments and Emerging Issues, by Tracey McDermott, 9 October, http://www.fca.org.uk/news/speeches/financial-services-regulation-enforcement.

Filippouli, E. (2013). Founder and CEO Global Thinkers Forum (GTF), www.globalthinkersforum.org.

Financial Times. (2009). Ideas Needed for a New Management Paradigm, by James Fleck. 21 September, http://www.ft.com/cms/s/0/cbacec96-a5f6-11de-8c92-00144feabdc0.html#axzz3OzJier3h.

Financial Times. (2012a). MBAs Need a Richer Educational Framework, by Bhaskar Chakravorti, 26 February, http://www.ft.com/cms/s/2/c1f32982-562e-11e1-8dfa-00144feabdc0.html#axzz3LPgVlXFe.

Financial Times. (2012b). Talent: No Stone Left Unturned in Hunt for Good Recruits, by Ross Tieman, 12 November, http://www.ft.com/cms/s/0/5479a580-22ab-11e2-8edf-00144feabdc0.html#axzz3LU3aOyLx.

Financial Times. (2012c). Although Daunting, Multi-school Partnerships are the Way Ahead, by Peter Brews, 26 November, http://www.ft.com/cms/s/2/60d56464-2a98-11e2-99bb-00144feabdc0.html#axzz3LU3aOyLx.

Financial Times. (2013). British Business Must Rebuild Public Trust – or be Forced to, by Richard Lambert, 25 October, http://www.ft.com/cms/s/0/5bb9512a-3bfe-11e3-b85f-00144feab7de.html#axzz3OzJier3h.

Financial Times. (2013a). Generation Next, by Emily Steel, 19 September, http://www.ft.com/cms/s/2/68707e76-204b-11e3-b8c6-00144feab7de.html#axzz3LPgVlXFe.

Financial Times. (2013b). India's MBA Dream Loses Some of its Lustre, by Avantika Chilkoti, 10 November, http://www.ft.com/cms/s/2/273bfc2a-4547-11e3-b98b-00144feabdc0.html#axzz3LU3aOyLx.

Financial Times. (2013c). No Room for Graduates as London Rents Soar, by Sarah O'Connor, 19 November, http://www.ft.com/cms/s/0/ef227e88-5115-11e3-b499-00144feabdc0.html#axzz3LPgVlXFe.

Financial Times. (2013d). Vehicle Innovators Face Fight to Win Hearts and Minds, by Henry Foy, 19 November, http://www.ft.com/cms/s/0/1d0056ec-f5ed-11e2-a55d-00144feabdc0.html#axzz3LU3aOyLx.

Financial Times. (2013e). The Future of European MBAs, by Emma Boyde, 1 December, http://www.ft.com/cms/s/2/b806fa28-512e-11e3-b499-00144feabdc0.html#axzz3LU3aOyLx.

Financial Times. (2013f). Ideas Adjust to New 'Facts' of Finance: Eight Ways Conventional Financial Wisdom Has Changed Post Crisis, by Gillian Tett, 26 December, http://www.ft.com/cms/s/0/a5d434b6-6e24-11e3-8dff-00144feabdc0.html#axzz3LbLZpjC5.

Financial Times. (2013g). Business Education and Public Policy Must Connect, by Mark Esposito, 15 December, http://www.ft.com/cms/s/2/c2b3aa62-46fb-11e3-9c1b-00144feabdc0.html#axzz3LbLZpjC5.

Finkelstein, D. (2013). The Big Society Lives on in Welby's Big Society Plan, *The Times*, 31 July.

Forster, E.M. (1910). *Howard's End*, Edward Arnold.

Freeman, R.E. (1984). *Strategic Management: A Stakeholder Approach*, Cambridge University Press.

Friedman, T. (2005). *The World is Flat: A Brief History of the 21st Century*, Farrar, Strauss and Giroux.

Fukuyama, F. (1990). *The End of History and the Last Man*, Free Press; Maxwell Macmillan Canada.

Fukuyama, F. (1995). *Trust: The Social Virtues and the Creation of Prosperity*, Free Press.

Gee, J.P. (1999). *An Introduction to Discourse Analysis: Theory and Method*, Routledge.

George, W. with Sims, P. (2007). *True North: Discover Your Authentic Leadership*, Jossey-Bass/Wiley.

Global Alliance for Public Relations. (2012). Mebourne Mandate: The Communicative Organisation, www.globalalliancepr.org.

Goleman, D. (1995). *Emotional Intelligence*, Business Books.

Gombrich, E.H. (1982). *The Image & The Eye*, Phaidon.

Gowing, N. (2009). *Sky Full of Lies and Black Swans: The New Tyranny of Shifting Information Power in Crisis*, Reuters Institute for the Study of Journalism.

Goyder, M. (2003). Redefining CSR: From Rhetoric of Accountability to the Reality of Earning Trust, Tomorrow's Company, www.tomorrowsco.com.

Graham, S. and Marvin, S. (2001). *Splintering Urbanism*, Routledge.

Gratton. L. (2014). *The Key: How Corporations Succeed by Solving the World's Toughest Problems*, McGraw-Hill.

Greenfield, S. (2014). *Mind Change: How Digital Technologies are Leaving Their Mark on the Brain*, Random House Publishing.

Grunig, J. and Grunig, L. (1992). *Excellence in Public Relations and Communication Management*, L. Erlbaum Associates.

Hall, P. (2013). *Good Cities, Better Lives, How Europe Discovered the Lost Art of Urbanism*, Routledge.

Handy, C.B. (2002). *The Age of Unreason*, Business Books.

Handy, C.B. (2003). *What is Business For?* HBR/Corporate Responsibility.

Hayes, R. (1997). *Systematic Networking: A Guide to Personal and Professional Success*, Cassells.

Hayes, R. (2012). Doctoral Dissertation, Henley Business School, University of Reading.

Hayes, R. and Watts, R. (1986). *Corporate Revolution: New Strategies for Executive Leadership*, Heinemann.

Hodge, R. and Kress, G. (1998). *Social Semiotics*, Polity Press.

Howells, R. (2003). *Visual Culture*, Polity Publishing.

Hudson, L. (2008). Leading and Supporting Strategic Collaborations. In *Engagement: Public Diplomacy in a Globalised World*, Foreign & Commonwealth Office, 146–59.

Hutton, W. (1995). *The State We're In*, Cape.

INSEAD. (2013). *What's at Stake?* Working Paper, INSEAD.

Institute for Public Relations. (2013). Authenticity and Employees, www.instituteforpublicrelations.com.

Jacobs, J. (1961). *The Death and Life of Great American Cities*, Vintage.

James, K. (2013). Speech at 'The Business of Changing the World', Institute for Public Relations Dinner, 21 November, New York, http://www.instituteforpr.org/wp-content/uploads/Gates-Kate-James-IPR-.pdf.

Jaworski, J. (2012). *Source: The Inner Path of Knowledge Creation*, Bernett-Koehler.

Johnson, S. (2012). *Future Perfect: The Case for Progress in a Networked Age*, Penguin.

King Report. (2009). Corporate Governance in South Africa, Professor Mervyn King, Institute of Directors, SA, www.iodsa.co.za.

Kjaer, A.L. (2013). Speech at European Commission, EUROSME, June 11–12, Dublin, Ireland.

Koch, R. and Lockwood, G. (2010) *Superconnect*, Abacus.

Kraus. M. (2006) Global Business Diplomacy: Raising the Bar, *Foreign Policy Magazine*, Council on Foreign Relations, Jan–Feb.

Kress, G. (1985). *Linguistic Processes in Sociocultural Practice*, Deakin University.

Kress, G. and Van Leeuwen, T. (1996). *Reading Images: The Grammar of Visual Design*, Routledge.

Mackey, J. and Sisodia, R. (2013). *Conscious Capitalism: Liberating the Heroic Spirit of Business*, Harvard Business Review Press.

Macleod, S. (2014). Sandra Macleod blog, www.mindfulreputation.com.

MacMillan, K., Money, K., Downing, S. and Hillenbrand, C. (2004). Giving Your Organisation Spirit: An Overview and Call to Action for Directors on Issues of Corporate Governance, Corporate Reputation and Corporate Responsibility. *Journal of General Management*, 30(2), 15.

McKinsey Insight Publications (50th Anniversary Edition). (2014). Leading Management Thinkers Tackle the Challenges of Tomorrow, *McKinsey Quarterly*.

McKinsey Quarterley. (2013/14). Strategy Articles & Insights, www.mckinsey.com.

Micklethwait, J. and Woolridge, A. (2000). *A Future Perfect: The Challenge and Hidden Promise of Globalisation*, Heinemann.

Naim, M. (2013). *The End of Power: From Boardroom to Battlefields*, Basic Books.

Nisbett, R. (2003). *The Geography of Thought: How Asians and Westerners Thinking Differently and Why*, Nicholas Brealey Publishing.

Nye, J. (2008). *The Powers to Lead*, Oxford University Press.

Oppel, W. (2007). The Global Leadership Challenge, *Regent Global Business Review*, May/June, 6–9.

Peters, T. and Waterman, R. (1982). *In Search of Excellence*, Harper and Row.

Phillips, R.A. and Reichart, J. (2000). The Environment as a Stakeholder? A Fairness-Based Approach, *Journal of Business Ethics*, 23(2), 185–97.

Plender, J. (1997). *A Stake in the Future*, Nicholas Brealey.

Porter, M. and Kramer, M. (2011). Creating Shared Value, *Harvard Business Review*, January–February, 2–17.

Prahalad, C.K. and Hammond, A. (2002) *Serving the World's Poor Profitably*, Allen.

Proust, M. (1922). *A la recherche du temps perdu*.

Putnam, R. (2000). *Bowling Alone: The Collapse and Revival of American Community*, Simon and Schuster.

Reputation Institute. (2013). Annual Reputation Leaders Survey, www.reputationinstitute.com.

Rometty, V. (2014). The World in 2014, The Year of the Smarter Enterprise, *The Economist*. www.economist.com/theworldin/2014.

Sachs, J. (2013). *To Move The World: JFK's Quest for Peace*, Random House.

Safdie, M. (1973). *Beyond Habitat*, The MIT Press.

Savitz, A., with Weber, K. (2006). *The Triple Bottom Line*, Jossey Bass/Wiley.

Sebeok, T.A. (1991). *A Sign is Just a Sign*, Indiana University Press.

Simm, S. (ed.) (1998). *The Icon Critical Dictionary of Postmodern Thought*, Icon Books.

Sunday Times. (2013). What I Learnt at Business School, by Carly Chynoweth, 8 December, http://www.thesundaytimes.co.uk/sto/business/business_education/article1349752.ece.

Taleb, N. (2007). *The Black Swan: The Impact of the Highly Improbable*, Random House.

Tapscott, D. (2012). *Wikinomics: Four Principles of the Open World*, Film.

The Economist. (2013a). Clever Cities: The Multiplexed Metropolis, http://www. economist.com/news/briefing/21585002-enthusiasts-think-data-services-can-change-cities-century-much-electricity.

The Economist. (2013b). The Butterfly Effect, 2 November, http://www. economist.com/news/business/21588853-charities-are-irritating-often-help-companies-do-right-thing-butterfly-effect.

The Economist. (2013c). After the Famine, by Lucy Kellaway, 18 November, http:// www.economist.com/news/21589123-prepare-feast-fads-after-famine.

The Economist. (2013d). It's Complicated: Management Thinkers Disagree on How to Manage Complexity, 23 November, http://www.economist.com/ news/business/21590341-management-thinkers-disagree-how-manage-complexity-its-complicated.

The Economist. (2013e). From Cuckolds to Captains: Corporate Boards are Playing a More Prominent Role in Steering Companies, 7 December, http://www. economist.com/news/business/21591166-corporate-boards-are-playing-more-prominent-role-steering-companies-cuckolds.

The Economist. (2013f). Temples of Delight, by Fiammetta Rocco, 21 December, http://www.economist.com/news/special-report/21591707-museums-world-over-are-doing-amazingly-well-says-fiammetta-rocco-can-they-keep.

Tichy, N. (2004). *Cycle of Leadership: How Great Leaders Teach Their Companies To Win*, Collins.

Tomorrow's Company. (2014). Annual Report, www.tomorrowscompany.com/ annualreport.

Vogel, D. (2008). Video on corporate responsibility, www.youtube.com.

Watras, M. (2014) CEO Straightline Inc., speech to J.P. Morgan Healthcare Conference, San Francisco, California, January.

Watts, R. (1970). *Reaching the Consumer*, Business Books.

Watts, R. (1972). *The Businessman's Guide to Marketing*, Business Books.

Welch, J. with Welch, S. (2005). *Winning*, Harper Collins.

Wheeler, D. and Sillanpaa, M. (1997). *The Stakeholder Corporation: A Blueprint for Maximising Stakeholder Value*, Pitman Publishing.

Williamson, J. (1978). *Decoding Advertisements: Ideology and Meaning in Advertising*, Marion Boyars.

World Economic Forum. (2012). The Role of Business – Global Agenda Council, www.wef.org.

Zadek, S. (2004). *The Civil Corporation: The New Economy of Corporate Citizenship*, Earthscan.

Zakaria, F. (2008, 2011, updated). *The Post American World*, Allen Lane.

Zolli, A. and Healy, A.M. (2012). *Resilience*, Headline Publishing Group.

Index

If you have found this book useful you may be interested in other titles from Gower

The Focused Organization
How Concentrating on a Few Key Initiatives Can Dramatically Improve Strategy Execution
Antonio Nieto-Rodriguez
Hardback: 978-1-4094-2566-3
e-book PDF: 978-1-4094-2567-0
e-book ePUB: 978-1-4094-5936-1

Corporate Strategy in the Age of Responsibility
Peter McManners
Hardback: 978-1-4724-2360-3
e-book PDF: 978-1-4724-2361-0
e-book ePUB: 978-1-4724-2362-7

Building Anti-Fragile Organisations
Risk, Opportunity and Governance in a Turbulent World
Tony Bendell
Hardback: 978-1-4724-1388-8
e-book PDF: 978-1-4724-1389-5
e-book ePUB: 978-1-4724-1390-1

Managing Responsibly
Alternative Approaches to Corporate Management and Governance
Edited by Jane Buckingham and Venkataraman Nilakant
Hardback: 978-1-4094-2745-2
e-book PDF: 978-1-4094-2746-9
e-book ePUB: 978-1-4094-6044-2

Visit **www.gowerpublishing.com** and

- search the entire catalogue of Gower books in print
- order titles online at 10% discount
- take advantage of special offers
- sign up for our monthly e-mail update service
- download free sample chapters from all recent titles
- download or order our catalogue

GOWER